Retirement Income
On The House

Cashing In

On Your Home

With A "Reverse" Mortgage

by Ken Scholen

NCHEC Press

National Center for Home Equity Conversion

Marshall, Minnesota

Copyright © 1992 by Ken Scholen

First Printing 1992

Printed and bound in the United States of America

All proceeds from the sale of this book support the work of the National Center for Home Equity Conversion, an independent, not-for-profit (501-C-3) organization (see page 340).

Library of Congress Catalog Card Number: 91-62233

ISBN 0-9630119-6-0

This book is designed to provide information on the subjects it covers. It is sold with the understanding that the author and publisher are not engaged in rendering legal, accounting, or other professional services. If legal or other expert assistance is required, the services of a competent professional should be sought. Although the author and publisher have made every effort to ensure the accuracy and completeness of the information contained in this book, they assume no responsibility for errors, inaccuracies, omissions, or inconsistencies.

To

Carol Arnold

and her 87 rosebushes

Table of Contents

Preface

Many retirees have dreamed of turning the equity in their homes into extra income.

Until recently, however, that has not been possible for most people. Their only choices were to sell their homes or take out home equity loans.

But selling means losing the security of home-ownwership - a place of your own with low carrying costs. And most "house-rich, cash-poor" homeowners don't have enough income to qualify for home equity loans. If they do, they usually are not eager to take on the obligation of a monthly loan repayment.

Over the past decade, a variety of experiments have been conducted for converting home equity into retirement income. This book explains these "reverse" mortgage plans in detail. Most of them require no repayment for as long as you live in your home.

For the past 13 years, author Ken Scholen has been in the vanguard of this consumer-led movement - urging lenders and legislators to develop useful programs, and educating consumers and their advisors about the risks and opportunities involved.

In this book, all his experience and knowledge come together in the most detailed and comprehensive guide to reverse mortgages you will find.

Having written about home equity conversion plans for many years, I know how difficult it has been to locate good information on them. That's why I know you'll find this book to be enormously useful.

It has taken many years and much effort to develop reverse mortgage lending. But, as you are about to learn, its time is finally at hand.

Jane Bryant Quinn
New York City   July 1, 1991

Acknowledgements

Everyone who pushes a rock up a hill should be so lucky.

For the past 13 years, it's been my good fortune to have worked with a wide array of talented, practical, persistent, and forward-looking people.

Sometimes it's embarrassing to admit just how long it has taken and how much effort has gone into developing these "reverse" mortgages. It's only as you near the top that you can see how far you've had to come.

There isn't enough room to acknowledge everyone who has brought us to this point. But I'd like to tell you about a few of the rock-pushers I've met along the way. Each has been ably assisted and supported by essential others.

It all started for me in the mid-1970s when I first heard retired homeowners talking about being "house-rich but cash-poor." Over the years, the never-ceasing and at times overwhelming interest of retirees has been the essential fuel for this movement. The thousands of homeowners who have shared their stories have also educated and informed the development process.

Standing with them have been consumer advocacy groups, led by the American Association of Retired Persons (AARP) Consumer Affairs Department, the American Bar Association Commission on Legal

Problems of the Elderly, and the United Seniors Health Cooperative. For most of the past decade, Katrinka Smith Sloan, Nancy Coleman, and James Paul Firman have piloted the leadership shown by these organizations in this area.

The idea of reverse mortgages owes much of its development to practical-minded scholars: Yung-Ping Chen was an early proponent of the concept at UCLA; Jack M. Guttentag produced the first rigorous technical analyses and product prototypes at The Wharton School; James A. Graaskamp (University of Wisconsin) provided inventive insights into marketing and design; Paul Samuelson (MIT) and Robert N. Butler (National Institute on Aging) contributed firm theoretical footings; Bruce Jacobs (University of Rochester) first explored the potential benefits for consumers and public policy; and Maurice Weinrobe (Clark University) gave us more than a decade's worth of seminal research and creative analysis that guided and shaped the overall development of the idea.

The best ideas can wither, however, without timely support. Critically important early supporters included Anita Miller at the Ford Foundation and the Federal Home Loan Bank Board, David Nee at the Florence V. Burden Foundation, Marilyn Hennessy at the Retirement Research Foundation, Kathryn Morrison at the U. S. Administration on Aging, and Dorcas Hardy at the U. S. Office of Human Development Services.

Providing vital counsel to individual consumers have been a variety of nonprofit and public sector service agencies. Don Ralya, Bronwyn Belling, and

Kathy Kenny created the first specialized reverse mortgage counseling service at the San Francisco Development Fund in 1981. That program led to the California Home Equity Conversion Coalition and helped start other pioneering programs ably led by Kay White in Arizona, Carol Greifer in New York, and Len Raymond in Massachusetts. These programs later served as models for the many counseling services developed through the FHA insurance program.

State officials have contributed breakthroughs in product design: Stuart Jennings and Arnold Pritchard developed the first "split-term" reverse mortgage in Connecticut; Robert Adams and Barry Merchant created the first creditline plan in Virginia.

The roll call of persons most responsible for important private sector "firsts" includes Arlo Smith, for the first formal reverse mortgage program; Trudy Ernst, for the first specialized legal documents; James Burke, for the historic first risk-sharing reverse mortgage; Peter Wessel, for the first equity preservation feature; William A. Phillips, for the first major corporate reverse mortgage; William Texido, for the first private creditline feature; David Maxwell, for the first secondary market program; and Jeffrey Taylor, for the first contract servicing program.

In the public policy arena, reverse mortgages have always had bipartisan support. The first Congressional hearings were held by Sen. John Heinz (R-PA) and Rep. Edward Roybal (D-CA). Other early supporters of the concept were Rep. Claude Pepper (D-FL) and Sen. Jake Garn (R-UT). The FHA program was championed by Sen. Bob Graham (D-FL) and Rep. George Wortley (R-NY). Key advocates over the years have been John Rother, Abbott Leban, James Broder, Rebecca Beauregard, Adelaide Attard, Jo Reed, Bonnie Caldwell, Philip Sampson, Donald Redfoot, Brian Lindberg, and Edward Cook.

The creativity and hard work that transformed a federal statute into a national reverse mortgage insurance program at FHA was spearheaded by Judith V. May of HUD's Division of Policy Development and Research. Some of her able teammates have been Edward J. Szymanoski, Jr., Mary Kay Roma, Patrick Quinton, Donald Alexander, and Sandy Krems. Their efforts have enjoyed the enthusiastic encouragement and support of HUD Secretary Jack Kemp.

My fulltime involvement with reverse mortgages since 1978 would not have been possible without the good counsel and support of Max Kummerow, James T. Sykes, and William C. Perkins. They taught me everything I know, and someday they'll have to answer for it.

The journey certainly would have been a lot less fun and much less productive without the friendship and skills of Bronwyn Belling. She's done it all, and most of it couldn't have happened without her.

And to Renee, Jonah, and Molly: thanks for letting me put off getting a real job till next year - 13 times!

Ken Scholen
Marshall, Minnesota   July 4, 1991

xii

Part
ONE

Getting
Started

Chapter 1

Questions

- ◆ Are you retired, or thinking about it?

- ◆ Do you own your home, and want to keep living there?

- ◆ Would you like more retirement income?

If your answers are "yes" this book is for you.

Most of us never cash in on our single most important investment. We live in our homes until we die. Because we do not sell and move, we do not get any cash return on our long-term investment in homeownership.

Until recently, you didn't have much choice. There were only two ways of turning your home into cash:

1) selling your home, or

2) borrowing against your home.

But that always used to mean selling *and moving*, or borrowing *and repaying every month*. Neither choice was very attractive if what you wanted was to stay in your home without having new monthly payments to make.

The two traditional methods of getting cash from your home just didn't work for most retired persons.

Now there is a third way.

"Reverse" Mortgages?

Reverse mortgages let you cash in on your home

☐ without giving it up, and

☐ without making monthly payments.

At first, that may *sound* like a good idea. But then, a lot of ideas that sound promising when you first meet them don't pan out.

On the other hand, a reverse mortgage just might turn out to *be* a good idea for you. At the very least, it raises a lot of immediate and important questions:

✓ How does it work?

✓ How much cash can you get?

✓ When can you get the cash?

✓ How much do these mortgages cost?

✓ What are the risks?

✓ Are there different *types* of reverse mortgages?

✓ Which type, if any, is best for you?

✓ What should you be looking for?

✓ What should you be looking *out* for?

Reverse mortgages may provide new financial opportunities. But you have to understand them before you can consider using them.

They may be a good idea for some people. But *you* need to do *your* homework before putting *your* home to work.

This Book

That's where this book comes in. It will help you

◆ *understand* reverse mortgages in general
(**Part TWO**),

◆ *analyze* any reverse mortgage program
(**Part THREE**),

◆ *examine* currently available plans
(**Part FOUR**), and

◆ *consider* if any reverse mortgage makes sense
for you (**Part FIVE**).

If you're eager to dive into the details of these mortgages, you may pass the rest of **Part ONE** and go directly to **Part TWO** (page 29). If you'd prefer to begin with some life-like examples of reverse mortgages in action, you may take a peek at the very last chapter (page 313).

But if you want to know more about these new loan plans in general before moving into the particulars, start with the next three short chapters:

☐ **Chapter 2**: a brief history of the idea;

☐ **Chapter 3**: some common first impressions;

☐ **Chapter 4**: a chapter-by-chapter road map to the rest of the book.

Chapter 2

Beginnings

Before you opened this book, you probably had heard or read something about reverse mortgages.

You even may have tried to find one. If you did, you probably were not successful. And if you were, you may not have found the type of reverse mortgage that fit your needs.

New financial products can be hardest to find when they first come out. That is also when they can be most difficult to understand, evaluate, and compare.

New products don't have much of a track record. There may not be a lot of different brands or models to choose from. And you often don't know anyone who has actually tried them.

It makes you wonder

◆ Just how new are they?

◆ Where did they come from?

◆ When will they be available all over?

◆ Will better models be coming out soon?

These are important questions. Being an informed consumer means more than understanding a group of currently available products. You also need a feel for the market as a whole: where it's come from, and where it might be going.

Most of this book is about reverse mortgages that are available today. But you also will learn how to analyze any reverse mortgage, and about the prospects for future development.

The rest of this chapter gives you a general look at where reverse mortgages have come from. You will find more details on the history of specific programs in later chapters.

An Idea Whose Coming Took Time

In the beginning, the *idea* of reverse mortgages made a big splash in the press. For a while, there were actually more articles being written about the concept than there were loans being made! You might have seen some of the many headlines:

"A Mortgage That Pays You"

"Reverse Mortgages Turn Equity Into Cash"

"Cashing In Without Moving On"

"Help Looms for 'House Rich, Cash Poor'"

"Tapping Equity for Retirement Income"

"Elderly Turn House Into Extra Cash"

"Cashing In On Your Paid-Up Mortgage"

"Making Equity Work for the Elderly"

"New Income for Paid-Up Homeowners"

"Unlocking the Cash Value of Your Home"

"Equity Plan Turns Home Into Pension"

"Reverse Mortgages Could Change Retirement"

The headlines started appearing in the early 1980s. And the basic concept was intriguing. Cash in on your home while you live in it. You paid for your home; now let it pay you.

A simple idea, but a powerful one. Hundreds of billions of dollars are tied up in the homes of older Americans. The home equity "nest egg" is the single largest financial asset of most retired persons. New ways of unlocking that value could provide important new opportunities for America's diverse and fast-growing elderly population.

Some were moved to say that the reverse mortgage was "an idea whose time has come." They should have added "but the reality will take a little longer."

Behind the Headlines

When the concept of reverse mortgages first hit the headlines, reverse mortgage lending was in its early infancy. Only a few experimental programs existed, and the first loan models were quite limited. Despite the bright promise of the idea, the reality was definitely "not ready for prime time."

In the early 1980s, there were only a handful of small reverse mortgage programs in the entire country. Most were sponsored by nonprofit or government agencies, and operated on a demonstration or test basis. It was extremely rare, therefore, that a homeowner could actually *find* one of these loans.

But that wasn't the only problem. The first reverse mortgages were not even designed to meet the needs of most homeowners.

The first public sector programs limited what you could use the loan for. The early private sector plans were not suited to most persons who expected to live in their homes for the rest of their lives. None of the programs gave borrowers much choice in arranging the loan's cash advances to fit their individual needs. And there was no way of protecting some of your equity for heirs or for other future uses.

In other words, the first reverse mortgages were highly specialized loans that raised more questions than they answered. Although they did a good job meeting the limited needs of some people, the early reverse mortgages simply did not make sense in most situations.

So - despite all the glowing headlines - most home-owners couldn't get a reverse mortgage. And most of those who *could* get one found that the early models didn't meet their needs.

Slow But Steady

During the 1980s, the reverse mortgage idea began to develop - slowly. Some of the loan plans become available throughout some states. More importantly, the design of the mortgages began to respond to a much wider range of consumer needs.

In particular, the newer reverse mortgages made sense for more persons expecting to remain in their homes indefinitely. And more consumer options began to appear: new choices for arranging the loan's cash advances, and for reserving equity for future use.

In 1988, a national survey found that most older homeowners were aware of reverse mortgages and thought they were a good idea. But you still couldn't find one in most states. And if you could, you probably didn't have more than one or two models to choose from.

Then, a new wave of development began that has continued into the present. It included a federal government program to insure reverse mortgages, major breakthroughs in loan design, and a number of key private sector initiatives.

At The Starting Gate - Finally

Today - more than a decade after those first headlines appeared - reverse mortgage borrowing is about to become a real option for most homeowners.

The federal reverse mortgage insurance program has just been made available to roughly 10,000 lenders nationwide. Increasingly, reverse mortgage programs offer an array of benefits and features that meet a wide range of consumer needs. And the first signs of large-scale investor interest have begun to appear.

At this point, however, more progress has been made on the design of reverse mortgages than on their availability.

Today's most feature-rich reverse mortgages offer many choices to consumers. Although some important new benefits may yet be added to them, these plans already provide great flexibility for tailoring benefits to individual needs.

But can you find one? All too often, the answer is still "no, not yet." But major forces newly afoot are beginning to expand availability on a broader scale than ever before. They are also making it easier for individual consumers and their advocates to persuade lenders to offer reverse mortgages.

Spearheaded by Consumers

Perhaps the most interesting part of the road to reverse mortgages has been the role of the consumer and the consumer advocate. Simply put, they have led the charge.

Individual consumers and organizations serving the elderly have consistently been the prime advocates for this new type of mortgage lending. They knew the need existed long before they or anyone else could figure out how to meet it.

They pushed for the first government-sponsored programs. They set up the first private, nonprofit programs. And they persuaded private sector lenders to establish their first small-scale programs.

Along the way, they heard all of the many reasons why it couldn't be done. But their knowledge of the need kept telling them there had to be a way. Over time, they chipped away at each of the technical and institutional barriers to reverse mortgages. Eventually, and one by one, the main roadblocks came tumbling down.

But Only If It Fits

You shouldn't draw any particular conclusions, however, from the fact that consumers have led the drive for reverse mortgages. It does *not* mean, for example, that any of these programs is officially endorsed by any consumer group. It also doesn't mean that any groups serving elderly consumers recommend that all homeowners should use reverse mortgages.

What it does mean is that consumer groups support the general idea of reverse mortgages. They believe it is in the interests of consumers that such loan plans are available. And they know that a reverse mortgage *can* be a good choice for *some* homeowners.

Whether or not a reverse mortgage *is* a good choice for *you* depends on the specific details of your individual situation, your personal preferences, and the types of reverse mortgages and other options that are available to you. The purpose of this book is to help you figure all of that out.

Chapter 3

First Impressions

Remember when you bought your first home? All those papers to sign? I'll never forget the look on the bank officer's face when I deadpanned, "Now this doesn't obligate us in any way, does it?"

Well of course it did. But when we signed that first mortgage to buy a home, we weren't the first ones ever to do so. We knew people who had done it before. And there were realtors and attorneys and accountants who knew all the ins and outs of "forward" mortgages.

We had learned just enough about mortgages to ask a few key questions. But we were most comforted by the fact that millions of others before us had done exactly the same thing - borrowed a lot of money to buy a home.

New Loans on the Block

Taking out a reverse mortgage today is quite a different story. It means being a pioneer, whether you want to be one or not.

If you were to take out a reverse mortgage now, you would no doubt be the first one on your block to do so. You also might be the first one in your neighborhood, town, or city.

It's much harder to make a major decision like this when you are at or near the front of the line. It makes you want to be "extra certain" that you're making the right choice.

There was a time when taking out a regular forward mortgage meant you had to be a pioneer. The very first persons to buy a home that way were also sailing into new waters:

- signing documents no one had seen before;

- living in a house long before it was paid for;

- taking on *thirty years* of monthly payments.

It wasn't long, though, before that mortgage plan became the standard. By now, it has helped several generations fulfill the American Dream of homeownership. But in the beginning, it was an untested financial product that few people fully understood.

First, Let's Tell All the Lawyers

Today, many professional advisors have little - if any - working knowledge of reverse mortgages. They can read up on these new loan plans - like you are. But it will be a while before they have built up a body of direct experience involving a range of different situations.

Some homeowners have been surprised to find that they know more about reverse mortgages than some attorneys, accountants, or financial planners do. That may not be very comforting. But it's not at all unusual at this time.

It makes you more cautious, however. Especially when these mortgages are so new and different.

Tilling New Soil

Reverse mortgages aren't just "new." They are fundamentally *different* from anything that's been available in the past. They let you do something that hasn't been done before.

Prior to reverse mortgages, getting cash from your home during retirement most often meant selling it and moving. If you stayed in your home, you usually didn't get any cash from it. Now you can do both at the same time: stay in your home, and get cash from it.

That's not just a new product or brand. It's a whole new way of thinking and acting - one that previous generations never knew. In some ways, it flies in the face of traditional patterns of thought and action.

For example, reverse mortgages can increase a homeowner's financial security. But how do we square that possibility with the sense of financial *insecurity* that has long been associated with debt against the family home?

A New Kind of Debt

Traditionally, the most compelling reason for avoiding debt against your home was to protect your ownership of it. Debt meant repayment. And if you missed a payment, you could lose your home.

By contrast, reverse mortgages are a new kind of debt. You don't have any monthly payments to make, so you can't miss one. *Some* of the traditional caution against borrowing on your home's equity, therefore, does not apply to reverse mortgage loans.

There are still plenty of good reasons to be careful, however. It's just that they are not the exact same set of reasons that apply to other types of borrowing against your home. After all, it is still your *home* we're talking about.

Where Your Equity Is

Perhaps the most obvious reason to take your time and be thorough about investigating reverse mortgages is that you have a lot at stake financially.

Your home may be your single largest and most important financial asset. Clearly, you want to make the best possible use of this major resource. You can't afford to make a mistake with it.

But your home is more than your "nest egg." It is also your "nest." It is the roof over your head, and the garden in your back yard. It gives you much of your sense of security, well-being, and independence.

What's It Worth To You?

You know your home, and the neighborhood and community of which it is a part. You know why you want to remain living in your home. You have probably even thought about how much it is worth to you to remain in your home.

A "forward" mortgage helped you buy your home. A reverse mortgage could help you keep it, get more out of it, or make it more enjoyable. It may even do so at a cost you are willing to pay.

But unless you understand the real costs and risks of reverse mortgage borrowing, you will not be able to evaluate them.

That's where this book comes in. So now let's look at our overall plan for exploring the world of reverse mortgages.

Chapter 4

This Book's For You

How thorough should you be about a decision that may be the most important one you make for the rest of your life?

Even if you're only casually looking at the possibility of a reverse mortgage, that question is a sobering one. At the very least, you should resolve to take your time and be as complete as you can.

This book will help you understand, analyze, and shop for reverse mortgages.

Understanding The Basics

Before getting into the specifics of any particular reverse mortgage program, you need to understand the basic shape and operation of these loan plans.

Some of this might seem simple and obvious. But you really do need to get these fundamentals firmly in mind.

If you have no background in banking or insurance, you may be better off than someone who does. It's the financial experts who are most likely to get these new-fangled loans confused with the types they already know so well.

Part TWO answers these questions:

☐ What is a reverse mortgage **(Chapter 5)**?

☐ How does it differ from a "forward" mortgage **(Chapter 6)**?

☐ What do the numbers look like **(Chapter 7)**?

☐ What are the main features of a reverse mortgage **(Chapter 8)**?

☐ How do lenders manage the risk involved in these loans **(Chapter 9)**?

☐ What are the different types of reverse mortgages **(Chapter 10)**?

Analyzing Reverse Mortgages

Part THREE shows you a simple method for analyzing any type of reverse mortgage.

That's especially important because it's likely that new plans will be appearing from time to time. If you know how to analyze them, you won't have to run off and buy later editions of this book.

Part THREE answers these questions:

- What does a reverse mortgage actually do **(Chapter 11)**?

- What can you get out of a reverse mortgage **(Chapter 12)**?

- What do they charge you for these loans **(Chapter 13)**?

- What do you actually end up paying for them **(Chapter 14)**?

- How much money do you have left at the end of the loan **(Chapter 15)**?

- How can you estimate the true and total cost of your loan **(Chapter 16)**?

- What should you be looking out for in these loans **(Chapter 17)**?

Reverse Mortgage Programs

Part FOUR takes the questions from Part THREE and applies them to each of the basic types of reverse mortgage currently being offered.

This shows you how to analyze specific programs and plans. It also introduces you to the particulars of each reverse mortgage now available.

Part FOUR examines the benefits and cost of each type of reverse mortgage. It also discusses who is eligible for them, and where you can get them.

Chapters 18 and 19 cover government-sponsored reverse mortgages for repairing homes and paying property taxes. **Chapter 20** looks at a simple type of uninsured private loan. **Chapters 21-23** analyze the new federally-insured reverse mortgage program. And **Chapter 24** considers the "lender-insured" private sector loan.

Shopping for Reverse Mortgages

Part FIVE applies what you have learned to your own situation.

Reverse mortgages sure are interesting, and they might be a good idea for some people. But do any of them make sense for you?

The starting point (**Chapter 25**) is your own situation: your needs, your resources, your choices, your plans. You need to understand these before you can consider what to do.

Chapter 26 looks at the options *other than* a reverse mortgage. Have you really considered other ways of meeting your needs? Have you missed a solution that does not involve using up your equity?

Chapter 27 reviews and compares the mortgages analyzed in Part FOUR. Which plans fit which situations? How do you compare similar plans?

Chapter 28 considers some of the financial consequences of reverse mortgage borrowing. Should you use your equity now or save it till later? How does the government treat the money you get?

Chapter 29 peers into the future. It looks at recent developments in light of ones that are about to unfold. Should you buy now, or wait a bit?

Chapter 30 presents a variety of fictional situations involving reverse mortgages. What issues are raised by each story? What would you do in each case?

Other Resources

The book concludes with appendixes, a glossary of terms, a resources section, and an index. You might take a peek at them now to see how they could be helpful to you as you wend your way through the pages ahead.

Part
TWO

Understanding
the Basics

Chapter 5

The Basic Definition

There are several different types of reverse mortgages, and the differences among them are important for you to understand.

But there are also some things that all reverse mortgages have in common. In this chapter, we look at the three most basic features that all reverse mortgages share.

A Three-Part Invention

A reverse mortgage is a loan

♦ against your *home* that

♦ gives you *cash*, and

♦ requires *no monthly repayments.*

As with most loans, you put up some security, you get some money, and you pay it back. But reverse mortgages are different in all three areas. Let's consider each part of this basic definition one at a time.

Home Equity

If you're like most people, you don't get loans based on your good looks. Lenders - for example, banks, savings and loan associations, credit unions - usually look for some other type of security. They need sounder reasons to believe that they will get back the money they lend you.

In a reverse mortgage, the lender is making a loan against the equity in your home. "Equity" or "home equity" simply means the value of your home minus any debt against it. For example, if you own a home worth $100,000 and still owe $20,000 on a regular "forward" mortgage, then you have $80,000 in home equity. If you own a home debt-free, then your equity is the same as the value of your home.

"Home Equity" Loans Aren't

"But," you might say, "that's not unusual. Lenders are eager to make home equity loans. I read about them in the paper all the time."

Well, those so-called "home equity" loans are *not* primarily loans against home equity. The lender is not looking chiefly to your equity for repayment. Instead, the lender is expecting to be repaid from your income.

This means you can qualify for a home equity loan only if the lender believes you have enough regular income to make the monthly repayments these loans require. If you miss a repayment, then the lender can look to your home as collateral. In other words, the lender can foreclose and sell the home to get repaid.

Reverse Mortgages Are

By contrast, reverse mortgages truly are loans against home equity - and *only* home equity.

This may seem like a minor technical point. But it is of major importance, because it means

✔ you do not need an income to qualify for a reverse mortgage;

✔ you do not have to make monthly payments on a reverse mortgage; and

✔ the lender can only look to your home's value for repayment (more on this later).

31

Cash Advances

Reverse mortgages provide cash to borrowers. The money you get goes by various names, and can be paid out to you in a variety of ways.

The words most often used to describe the money you get are "cash advances" or "loan advances." Sometimes they are called "payments." (But you have to remember that these are payments from the lender to you - not the other way around.) A more technical name for a loan advance is a "disbursement."

It's not so important what you call the advances. What is important is how the money is paid out to you. Here are some of the choices available in some reverse mortgage plans:

☐ a single "lump sum" of cash when you take out the loan, that is, upon "closing" the loan;

☐ monthly advances for as long as you live in your home;

☐ monthly advances for a definite time period;

☐ a "line-of-credit" that lets you decide how much money to get, and when to get it; or

☐ any combination of these choices, for example, a lump sum at closing plus a monthly advance plus a line-of-credit.

No Repayment

Like all loans, a reverse mortgage must be repaid. The difference lies in when you must repay it.

Regular monthly loan repayments are not required on any reverse mortgage. If you choose, however, you may generally repay part or all of the loan at any time without penalty.

Most reverse mortgages do not require repayment of any kind for as long as you or any co-borrower live in your home. When you die, sell your home, or permanently move, then you or your estate must repay all the loan advances you have received plus interest.

In some reverse mortgages, you must repay the loan on a specific date that you and the lender agree upon at loan closing. This used to be the only type of private sector reverse mortgage. Today, not many of these programs are still around.

Quick Recap

Reviewing the basics: a reverse mortgage is

✓ a loan made against your *home equity*

✓ that gives you *cash advances*

✓ and requires *no repayment* until a future time.

Chapter 6

Forward and Reverse

A good way to see the basic shape of a reverse mortgage is to compare it with a regular "forward" mortgage - the loan you use to buy a home.

This chapter does so in two ways: first, it looks at stages in the "life" of each type of mortgage; second, it compares their basic purposes. Chapter 7 fills out the story with some numbers and pictures.

By the time these two chapters are over, you may have had your fill of mortgage comparisons. But take your time and stick with it. It'll give you several views of how reverse mortgages are different from other types of loans. And that will come in handy later on.

You'd be amazed how easy it is to forget some of the basic differences between reverse mortgages and other loans. Seeing the distinctions clearly now will make everything easier later.

Scenes from a Mortgage

You are living in an apartment, saving for a down-payment. You want a place of your own, and you want to start building up some equity. You find a house, make an offer to purchase, and take out a regular "forward" mortgage.

Now you have the privilege of making monthly loan payments for the next thirty years. It seems like forever. But, one way or another, you do it. You pay off the mortgage, and you own your home free and clear of any debt.

Sound familiar? Probably does. But think about the basic developments in this story. You start with no equity and a substantial debt. Over time, you make monthly payments on your loan, thereby reducing the amount of your debt. Meanwhile, the value of your home is probably growing.

Falling Debt, Rising Equity

The result is that your equity (that is, the value of your home minus any debt against it) increases over time. Eventually, you have no remaining debt and substantial equity in your home. That is why we call the forward mortgage a *"falling debt, rising equity"* type of deal (see **Table 1**).

Play It Again - Backwards

Now - many years later - you own a home free and clear of debt. You want to convert your equity into cash without having to leave your home, and without having to make monthly loan repayments.

You hear about reverse mortgages, and read this book. Still interested, you investigate all your options and consider them carefully. You take your time, and you consult people you trust.

Finally, you conclude that a certain type of reverse mortgage fits your needs. You decide to turn your equity into a monthly income that will be paid to you for as long as you live in your home.

Rising Debt, Falling Equity

In the reverse mortgage story, you start with no debt and substantial equity. Over time, you get loan advances from the lender and you make no repayments. As a result, the amount you owe goes up.

Table 1: Comparison of Typical "Forward" and
          Reverse Mortgages

	"Forward" Mortgage	Reverse Mortgage
Purpose of the loan:	to purchase a home	to create income
Before closing, you have . . .	no equity	a lot of equity
After closing, you . . .	owe a lot, and have little equity	owe very little, and have a lot of equity
During the loan, you . . .	make monthly payments to the lender; your debt goes down and your equity rises	receive monthly advances from the lender; your debt rises and your equity goes down
At the end of the loan, you . . .	owe nothing, and have a lot of equity	owe a lot, and have little or no equity

The longer your loan runs, the more you owe. And as your debt rises, the amount of equity you have left in your home usually goes down (unless your home's value is growing very fast). That is why we call the reverse mortgage a *"rising debt, falling equity"* type of deal (see **Table 1**).

When you die, sell your home, or permanently move, the loan is over. You or your estate must then pay back what you owe all at once. Particularly if your loan has run a long time, your debt could be a substantial amount. It is possible that you or your heirs would have little if any equity remaining.

At Cross Purposes

Reverse mortgage borrowers use debt for different reasons than forward mortgage borrowers do.

In a reverse mortgage, you turn your equity into income. In a forward mortgage, you turn your income (via monthly loan repayments) into equity. In a reverse mortgage, you "spend down" the equity you used a forward mortgage to build up. You put the forward mortgage "in reverse."

Because these loans have different purposes, they work differently. In a forward mortgage you borrow a large amount of cash at closing, and then pay it back in smaller amounts month-by-month over many years.

In a reverse mortgage, you typically borrow smaller amounts of cash (often month-by-month) over many years, and then pay it back with a large amount of cash at the end of the loan.

That's the basic idea. In the next chapter we'll take a look at some specific numerical examples. We'll also see what reverse mortgages look like when we turn them into graphs.

Chapter 7

Once More With Numbers

Now that you've got a general sense of how these loans work, let's consider some simple examples.

In the last chapter, Table 1 presented a side-by-side comparison of the various stages in the lives of forward and reverse mortgages. In this chapter, **Table 2** adds some numbers to those stories. After you look at them, we'll draw some pictures of these loans, and then show you where the numbers came from.

In both of the mortgages in **Table 2,** we assume the home is worth an even $100,000 at closing, that the loan runs for 15 years, and that it has an interest rate of 10%. To keep things simple at this stage, we leave out all loan fees and other charges.

In the forward mortgage, we assume you make a downpayment of $10,000 and borrow the rest of the money needed to buy the home ($90,000). During the loan, you pay back about $967 every month. After 15 years, you have paid back about $174,000, of which about $84,000 has been interest.

Now you own your home free and clear of debt. If your home's value has grown (that is, appreciated) by 4% each year, it is now worth about $180,000.

You have turned a $10,000 downpayment and $967 of monthly income over 15 years into $180,000 in home equity. You have done so using a "falling debt, rising equity" type of mortgage.

Reversing the Numbers

In the reverse mortgage, we assume you start off owning your home debt-free. To keep things simple for now, we also assume that you select a plan that gives you a cash advance every month for as long as you live in your home.

This plan does not include a lump sum of cash at closing, and it does not include a line-of-credit account.

Table 2: Examples of "Forward" and Reverse Mortgages
at 10% Interest Over 15 Years*

	"Forward" Mortgage	Reverse Mortgage
AT LOAN CLOSING		
Value of home	$100,000	$100,000
Equity ** in home	$10,000	$100,000
Loan advance	$90,000	0
DURING THE LOAN		
Monthly advance	0	$350
Monthly repayment	$967	0
AFTER 15 YEARS		
Amount repaid	$174,000	0
Amount owed	0	$146,000
Equity*** after loan is paid off	$180,000	$34,000

*Calculated figures are rounded off

**Assumes the forward mortgagor makes a $10,000 downpayment, and the reverse mortgagor owns the home debt-free

***Assumes a 4% annual average rate of home appreciation over 15 years

During this reverse mortgage, you receive a monthly loan advance of $350 - and you make no monthly repayments. Over 15 years you receive $63,000 in monthly advances (180 months times $350).

If you or your estate pay back the loan at the end of 15 years, you owe that $63,000 plus about $83,000 in interest for a total of about $146,000. If your home's value has appreciated at a rate of 4% each year, it is now worth about $180,000.

You have now turned $100,000 in home equity into cash advances of $350 per month for 15 years - with $34,000 in equity left over. You have done so using a "rising debt, falling equity" type of mortgage.

Worth How Many Words?

But what do these mortgages look like? Exactly how do the debt and equity "rise" and "fall" - and vice versa? **Charts 1-2** are pictures of the two mortgages you met in Table 2.

Forward Mortgage

The bars in **Chart 1** represent the value of your home over time. Reading from left to right, you can see that it starts at $100,000 at closing ("K" means $1,000; so 100K equals $100,000). Over the next 15 years, the value increases to about $180,000. (If you guessed that's an appreciation rate of 4% per year, you're right on target.)

Now look at the shaded lower part of each bar. It represents the amount of debt against the property. At closing, it comes up to the $90,000 mark. Over time it drops to zero. You could call it "falling debt."

The unshaded top part of each bar is your equity (home value minus debt). In the beginning, it equals your $10,000 downpayment. But over the course of the loan it increases as your home's value rises and your debt falls. You could call it - all together now - your "rising equity."

Remember, the basic storyline of a forward mortgage is simply "falling debt, rising equity."

Chart 1: Example of a Forward Mortgage at 10% Interest Over 15 Years (4% Home Appreciation)

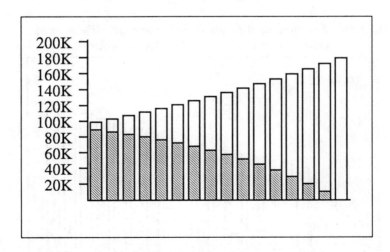

Reverse Mortgage

As in Chart 1, the bars in **Chart 2** represent your home's value, which starts at $100,000 and increases (we assume) to about $180,000 after 15 years.

But notice how different the debt pattern is with a reverse mortgage. The debt - represented by the shaded lower part of each bar - is lowest in the early years. But it increases at an ever increasing rate.

You keep getting loan advances. More and more interest is added to your loan balance. And you make no repayments. That's how your "rising debt" rises.

But as the debt eats up more of your home's value, your remaining equity gets smaller. The unshaded top part of each bar - your equity - decreases every year. And that's how your "falling equity" falls.

Chart 2: Example of a Reverse Mortgage at 10% Interest Over 15 Years (4% Home Appreciation)

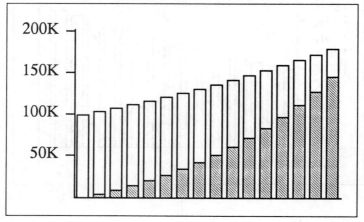

Summary

The basic differences between traditional forward mortgages and the new reverse mortgages have to do with income, debt, and equity.

In the forward mortgage you use your income to pay off your debt, and that gives you equity. In the reverse mortgage, you use your equity to create debt, and that gives you income. In each case you use what you have to get what you need.

Columns Aplenty

If you've been waiting patiently for columns of numbers, wait no more. They aren't as complicated as they're going to be in later chapters, but they should hold you for a while.

If, on the other hand, you've been dreading the columns, take comfort. We'll go slowly and focus on the key items. Besides, you can always turn back to Charts 1 and 2 to see how the columns of numbers look and behave.

Tables 3 and 4 show the year-by-year details of the sample loans that were summarized in Table 2 and graphed in Charts 1 and 2.

Table 3 presents the forward mortgage details, and Table 4 presents the reverse mortgage details. The assumptions are the same as in Table 2 and Charts 1 and 2.

Forward the Details

Table 3 shows you once again that the forward mortgage is indeed a "falling debt, rising equity" loan. Notice that at the beginning of the loan ("end of year 0"), you have high debt ($90,000) and low equity ($10,000). By the end of year 15, you have no debt and high equity ($180,094).

How does this happen? During the first year of the loan, you pay off $2,728 of your $90,000 principal debt, reducing your loan balance to $87,272. (Looks suspiciously like "falling debt.")

Also in the first year, we assume that your home's value increases by 4% to $104,000. Subtracting your new, lower loan balance from this higher home value, you can see that you home equity has now risen to $16,728.

Reading down the table, you see that this keeps happening year after year. More and more of your repayments go toward reducing your principal balance each year. If you read down the column headed "Loan Balance," you see the debt falling at an ever faster rate.

Meanwhile, your home's value is growing, and so is your equity ("Home Value @ 4%" minus "Loan Balance" equals "Home Equity"). If you read down the "Home Equity" column, you see the equity rising at an ever faster rate. By the end of the forward mortgage, your debt (loan balance) has fallen to zero, and your equity has risen to about $180,000.

Table 3: Details of Sample Forward Mortgage; $90,000 at 10% Interest Over 15 Years

End Year	Principal Paid	Interest Paid	Loan Balance	Home Value @ 4%	Home Equity
0	-0-	-0-	$90,000	$100,000	$10,000
1	$2,728	$8,877	87,272	104,000	16,728
2	5,743	17,469	84,257	108,160	23,903
3	9,073	25,745	80,927	112,486	31,559
4	12,751	33,672	77,249	116,986	39,737
5	16,815	41,214	73,185	121,665	48,480
6	21,303	48,330	68,696	126,532	57,836
7	26,263	54,977	63,737	131,593	67,856
8	31,742	61,104	58,258	136,857	78,599
9	37,794	66,657	52,206	142,331	90,125
10	44,480	71,577	45,520	148,024	102,504
11	51,866	75,796	38,134	153,945	115,811
12	60,026	79,242	29,974	169,103	130,129
13	69,040	81,834	20,960	166,507	145,547
14	78,998	83,482	11,002	173,167	162,165
15	90,000	84,087	0	180,094	180,094

KEY: "End Year" means end of year (0 = closing). "Principal Paid" means the amount of the borrower's total monthly payments to date that have been used to pay off the $90,000 debt. "Interest Paid" means the amount of the borrower's total monthly payments to date that have been used to pay off the interest on the $90,000 debt. "Loan Balance" means the amount owed; it equals $90,000 minus the "principal paid." "Home Value @ 4%" means the amount the home is worth based on the assumption that it increases in value by 4% each year. "Home Equity" means the value of the home minus the amount still owed, that is. "Home Value @ 4%" minus "Loan Balance."

Reverse the Details

The basic thing to see in **Table 4** is that the reverse mortgage is indeed a "rising debt, falling equity" loan. At loan closing ("end of year 0"), you have no debt and $100,000 in equity. By the end of year 15, your debt has risen to about $146,000, and your equity has fallen to about $34,000.

You can see it beginning to happen in the very first year. You receive $4,200 in loan advances ($350 times 12 months), and the lender charges you $235 in interest for a total loan balance of $4,435. But as your debt has risen, your equity has begun to fall. At the end of the first year, your equity stands at $99,565, assuming your home's value increases by 4% during the year..

Reading down the table, you see these two movements pick up speed. As you get more loan advances and more interest is added to your loan balance (including interest on the interest already added), your debt grows at an ever increasing rate. If you read down the column headed "Loan Balance," you can see how your rising debt rises.

Meanwhile, although your home's value may be rising, it probably isn't doing so fast enough to keep your equity rising. At the 4% annual home appreciation rate assumed in Table 4, your equity drops to about $34,000 at the end of 15 years. You can see your equity fall year-by-year reading down the column headed "Home Equity."

Table 4: Details of Sample Reverse Mortgage;
$350 Per Month at 10% Interest Over 15 Years

End Yr	Loan Advances	Interest	Loan Balance	Home Value @ 4%	Home Equity
0	-0-	-0-	-0-	$100,000	$100,000
1	$4,200	$235	$4,435	104,000	99,565
2	8,400	936	9,336	108,160	98,824
3	12,600	2,146	14,746	112,486	97,740
4	16,800	3,924	20,724	116,986	96,262
5	21,000	6,329	27,329	121,665	94,336
6	25,200	9,424	34,625	126,532	91,907
7	29,400	13,285	42,685	131,593	88,908
8	33,600	17,990	51,590	136,857	85,267
9	37,800	23,626	61,426	142,331	80,905
10	42,000	30,293	72,293	148,024	75,731
11	46,200	38,098	84,298	153,945	69,647
12	50,400	47,160	97,560	160,103	62,543
13	54,600	57,610	112,210	166,507	54,297
14	58,800	69,594	128,394	173,167	44,773
15	63,000	83,273	146,273	180,094	33,821

KEY: "End Yr" means end of year (0 = closing). "Loan Advances" means the total of all monthly cash advances received by the borrower to date ($350 per month). "Interest" means all the interest charged on those loan advances but not yet paid by the borrower, that is "interest accrued." "Loan Balance" means the amount owed; it equals the "Loan Advances" plus the "Interest." "Home Value @ 4%" means the amount the home is worth based on the assumption that it increases in value by 4% each year. "Home Equity" means the value of the home minus the amount still owed, that is. "Home Value @ 4%" minus "Loan Balance."

Questions Rush In

As soon as you look at specific numerical examples, the questions start to flow.

The most important ones involve the assumption that your home's value will grow at 4% per year. We will examine various aspects of that issue in coming chapters.

But we also need to complete our introduction to the general concept of reverse mortgage loans. In the last three chapters of **Part TWO**, you will learn

✓ the other main features of these loans,

✓ how lenders manage the risk in these loans, and

✓ the basic types of reverse mortgages.

Chapter 8

The Main Features

A reverse mortgage - as you learned in Chapter 5 - is a loan made against your *home equity* that gives you *cash advances* and requires *no repayment* until a future time.

Those are the three most basic features that all reverse mortgages share. In this chapter we go on to consider the other main features that these loans have in common. And yes, you will hear just a bit more about "rising debt" and "falling equity."

Keeping Your Title

When you take out a reverse mortgage, you do not give up ownership of your home.

You keep the title to your property, and all the privileges that go with it. You know, making repairs, doing maintenance work, paying property taxes and homeowner's insurance.

The lender does not get any ownership rights. You continue to be the owner just like when you had a forward mortgage.

Just Like a Forward

When you were making forward mortgage payments to the lender, it might have *felt* like the bank "owned" your home. But in fact, the title was in your name. And as long as you made your payments, paid your taxes, and kept your home in reasonable condition, your ownership rights were safe.

In a reverse mortgage, you do not have to make monthly payments to the lender. But you do have to pay your property taxes and keep up your property - just as you do in a forward mortgage.

The lender does not have an ownership interest in your home. But the lender does have a creditor interest. This means the loan must be paid off before anyone else can become the owner. The lender does not "get" your home when you die or sell.

Sizing Up Your Advances

How much cash can you get from a reverse mortgage?

That will depend to a large extent on the type of reverse mortgage you choose, and the kind of loan advances you select. But in general, the amount will depend on factors such as your age, the value of your home, and the cost of the loan.

As you will see in later chapters, the oldest borrowers with the most valuable homes and the lowest loan costs generally get the greatest loan advances. On the other hand, the youngest borrowers with the least valuable homes and the highest loan costs get the smallest loan advances.

Financing the Fees

The various loan fees and other non-interest costs of reverse mortgages are especially important for you to understand.

They come in many shapes and sizes. Chapter 13 looks at the range of possibilities. Chapters 18-24 consider the cost of specific plans in detail.

But for now, you need to know that in most cases these costs can be "financed." In other words, they can be paid for by the loan advances.

For example, if the cost of setting up a loan is $3,000, then the first loan advance can include $3,000 for paying these costs. This means that there is no cash, out-of-pocket cost for setting up the loan.

No Cash Out Of Pocket

That doesn't mean the loan will be "free," although it could end up that way. It just means that you don't have to have any cash - or use any of the cash you do have - to set up a reverse mortgage.

The $3,000 loan advance you use to pay the loan costs is added to your loan balance. And interest is charged on that amount for as long as the loan runs. You still are required to pay it back, and you may or may not actually end up doing so. More on that later.

In many cases, financing your loan costs will turn out to be a wise choice. We'll take a closer look at this issue in Chapter 14.

Noting the Exceptions

By now you know that a reverse mortgage is a "rising debt, falling equity" type of loan.

But you may also recall a suggestion that a *rapidly* increasing home value might actually result in *rising* equity. Let's take a minute to look at exceptions to the general rule of "rising debt, falling equity."

Chart 3 shows the same mortgage we saw last chapter in Chart 2. It provides $350 per month at 10% interest, and we assume it runs for 15 years. So the rising pattern of debt (the lower shaded portion) is the same as in Chart 2.

But in this case the home's value rises at 8% per year - twice as fast as the appreciation in Chart 2. So the bars get taller faster. And the unshaded top part of each bar - your equity - actually *increases* over time in this example: a "rising debt, rising equity" reverse mortgage.

Some homes have appreciated at this or even higher rates in some areas in the past. In recent years, however, we have seen that what goes up can come down, especially in the short run.

Chart 3: Example of a Reverse Mortgage at 10% Interest Over 15 Years (8% Home Appreciation)

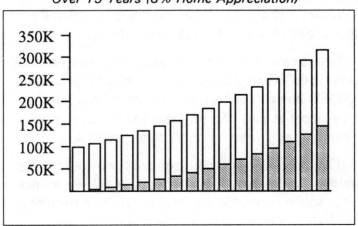

A Conservative Surprise

You certainly don't want to over-estimate the amount of equity that will be remaining at any given point.

You know for certain that a reverse mortgage uses up home equity. What you can't know for certain is how your home's value will change and, therefore, how much equity will be left in the future.

Better to under-estimate home appreciation and be pleasantly surprised than the other way around.

Chapter 16 includes a discussion of future appreciation rates. To suggest the range of possibilities, rates of 0%, 4%, and 8% are used throughout this book.

On Its Head

Chart 4 shows a reverse mortgage in which the debt doesn't rise at all - and then it drops.

In this case, the borrower takes out a lump sum of cash ($10,000) at closing to make major repairs on a $60,000 home. The loan is made by a local housing department as part of a program to encourage low-income homeowners to repair their properties.

The incentive for the borrower is two-fold: 1) there are no interest charges on the loan, and 2) the principal advance is completely forgiven if the borrower is still living in the home after 10 years.

Chart 4: Example of a Zero-Interest, "Forgivable" Reverse Mortgage

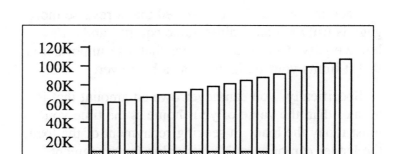

In Chart 4, note that the debt (the shaded lower part of each bar) remains the same until the end of the tenth year. The loan balance does not rise because there is only one loan advance, and there is no interest charged on it.

After not rising for 10 years, the debt disappears altogether. Meanwhile, the home continues to appreciate at an assumed 4% per year.

The overall result is a "falling debt, rising equity" reverse mortgage. Just the opposite of the general rule.

So it is possible that a reverse mortgage can be something other than a "rising debt, falling equity" loan. It really depends on the specific facts of each case. But for the most part, loans that charge interest and require no repayment will be rising-debt loans.

Limiting Your Liability

Back in Chapter 5, you learned that a reverse mortgage is truly a loan against home equity - and *only* home equity. One of the reasons that's so important is that it limits your obligations as a borrower.

Specifically, you can never owe an amount that is greater than the value of your home at the time you must repay the loan. In seeking repayment of the loan, the lender can only look to its value for repayment.

The technical term for this is a "non-recourse" limit. In other words, the lender does not have legal recourse to anything other than the home's value. The lender cannot resort to seeking repayment from your income, your other assets, or from your heirs.

This important consumer safeguard protects you, your estate, and your heirs from "deficiency judgments," that is, from ever being required to repay more than the value of your home.

How Can They Do That?

A nice safeguard, you say. But how can they do that?

Isn't it possible that a loan balance could grow very large if a borrower lived a very long time? And isn't it possible that a home's value could fail to grow - or even fall?

What if both of those things happened on the same loan? Wouldn't the lender stand to lose a lot of money on a "non-recourse" loan? How could a lender manage to take such a heavy loss?

These questions are important ones. The answers tell you much about the risks of reverse mortgage lending and borrowing. And this helps you see the basic structure and cost of these loans.

That's why the whole next chapter is devoted to these questions. If you want to understand reverse mortgages, you need to look at the risks.

Chapter 9 shows you how lenders manage the risk of losing money on reverse mortgages.

Chapter 9

Managing Risk

"Risk management" sounds complicated. But you do it all the time. For the most part, it's just plain common sense.

How do you manage the risk that your house might burn down? That you might be in a car accident? That you might have a heart attack? That someone might be injured on your property?

You Risk Manager, You

You are already managing a variety of risks. You do so in three basic ways:

1) you educate yourself about the causes of the risks, or the "risk factors";

2) you take action to remove the causes or cut down on the risk factors; and

3) you take out insurance policies to "spread out" or share the risk among a larger group.

For example, you've learned a lot over the years about fire prevention, auto safety, heart disease, and household accidents. No doubt you've used that knowledge about the causes of these problems to reduce the risk factors in each area.

Maybe you've bought a smoke alarm, started buckling up, watched your diet, or installed a railing. The purpose of these risk reduction activities is to make it less likely that you will run into trouble, and cut down on the amount of any trouble you do meet.

Insurance, What A Concept

You no doubt also have insurance policies of one type or another. Their purpose is to help you cope with the financial cost of any "insured" trouble you meet. You and all the other insured persons pay cash premiums to the insurance company. Whichever of you meets up with trouble gets a cash payment or "benefit" from the company. In that way, the risk is "spread out" or shared among a larger group of people. You all pay in, but you only get something back if you meet trouble.

If you don't meet trouble, you don't get any cash benefits. What you do get, however, is protection against risk, or "coverage." This means that the risks are covered by the insurance. In other words, if you meet "covered" trouble, you get cash benefits.

In fact, however, you are hoping you won't get any cash benefits because you can only get them if you meet trouble first. Ideally, you want to get great coverage at an outstanding price - but never collect any cash benefits.

So, you see, you really do know quite a bit about "risk management." You pay attention to risk factors, you try to cut them down or out, and you take out insurance policies to spread your risks over a larger group of insured persons.

Now let's apply what you already know about managing risk to reverse mortgages.

Understanding the Risk

For the lender, the central risk in a reverse mortgage is that the home will not be worth enough to pay back all the loan advances that have been made plus all the interest that has been charged.

This can happen if the home's value grows less than expected (appreciation risk), or if the borrower lives longer than expected (mortality risk).

Sample Losses

Recall the sample reverse mortgage you looked at in Chapter 7. Remember? It provided $350 per month for as long as you lived in your home. If you paid it back after 15 years, the total of all loan advances plus interest was $146,000.

At that time your home - which we *assumed* to be appreciating at 4% per year - was worth about $180,000. So there was enough value to pay back the loan, with about $34,000 in equity left over.

But what if the home's value did *not* grow at a rate of 4% per year? What if the home did not appreciate at all? Then it would still be worth $100,000 after 15 years. And that's $46,000 *less* than the total of all loan advances plus interest.

Necessary Losses?

Because of the non-recourse limit on the loan, you would only be liable for $100,000. That means the lender would realize a $46,000 loss.

If you lived another 10 years, continued to get $350 each month, and your home still did not appreciate, the losses would become even greater.

How can lenders do that? What would make them able to take on such risk?

Reducing the Risk

Some lenders manage the risk of loss simply by limiting the amount of cash advanced. If the limits are strong, then the risk is low. The tighter the limits, the lower the risk will be. Here are three examples.

Three Risk Reduction Plans

A lender could permit only one-time, lump sum loans. You get a chunk of money at closing, but that's all you ever can get. This single advance could be limited to, say, 20% of the home's value. That would give the lender a big 80% "cushion" against losses.

Another approach could be to permit more than one advance, but to keep the advances small and far apart. For example, each advance could be limited to one or two per cent of the home's value, and you could be limited to no more than one advance per year.

To make this second type of mortgage even safer for the lender, the loan agreement could also limit the total amount of all of these yearly advances put together. When this overall amount is reached, no more annual advances would be permitted.

Still another approach could be to provide monthly advances, but to limit both the amount and number of such advances, and to require repayment in full on a specific date. The amount and number could be set so that the loan balance could not grow larger than some percentage of the home's value at closing.

Consumer Drawbacks

In fact, each of these three approaches is currently being used by various reverse mortgage lenders (see Chapters 18-20).

These risk reduction methods represent some of the earliest attempts to manage the risk of loan losses. Each has the goal of preventing loss on every individual reverse mortgage loan. There is no sharing of risk among all the loans in these programs.

These methods do a good job of reducing risk for lenders. They do it by sharply limiting the loan advances to borrowers. That gives the lender a large cushion against loss on every loan.

But it also makes these types of reverse mortgages much less attractive to most consumers.

Meeting Consumer Needs

You might need a lump sum of cash larger than 20% of your home's value. You might prefer the security of a monthly advance that continues for as long as you live in your home. You might want a line-of-credit that you can use when and how you choose.

These needs could not be met by loans using only the risk reduction methods described above.

So how do lenders do it? How can they make the more useful and flexible kinds of reverse mortgages? Simply put, they take the next risk management step. In addition to risk reduction, they use risk sharing.

Sharing the Risk

The basic idea is a familiar one. You spread out the risk that any reverse mortgage will suffer a loss over a whole group of them.

You do this in the same general way you do in other insurance programs. You charge an insurance premium on every loan, and put that money aside. Then, when losses do occur, you use that money to cover them.

In this way, the premiums of the many are used to cover the losses of the few. Not everyone's loan has a loss. But everyone's premiums are used to pay for the ones that do.

To keep the loss risk low, various risk reduction methods are also used. They are based on the specific risk factors involved: appreciation and mortality.

Analyzing the Risk

Now let's see how the basic idea of risk sharing works when it's applied to reverse mortgages. To make this a little more interesting, let's pretend that *you* are the executive who has been given the job of figuring out how to insure reverse mortgages.

What do you do? You hire a consultant, and ask for recommendations. Specifically, you ask for a plan that lets borrowers get monthly cash advances for as long as they live in their homes. Then you set up a meeting date to hear the consultant's report. Piece of cake.

Report # 1 - Too "Generous"

The meeting date arrives. The consultant tells you that consumers will be very reluctant to borrow against their homes, and the program must be made extremely generous to them:

> Therefore we recommend, for example, that a 65-year-old couple living in a $60,000 home should get cash advances of $2,000 every month for as long as either of them shall live in their home.

Let's see. That's $24,000 per year! Why, at that rate, the loan would lose money for sure - and lots of it. In only three years, the loan advances alone (not counting interest) would be $72,000 - on a $60,000 home.

And the odds are that at least one spouse will live for 20 years. By that time, the loss on this single loan would be through the roof.

If all your loans were set up to be this generous, almost all of them would lose large amounts of money. On the few loans that did not lose money, you couldn't charge enough of a premium to make up for the losses. This "extremely generous" plan simply would not work.

So you fire the consultant. You obviously know more about it by far. But you're still not clear how to proceed. So you hire a second consultant. This time, however, you make it clear that "extremely generous" reverse mortgages are not the answer. They would make any lender "extremely broke."

Report # 2 - Too "Careful"

The new consultant has listened well, and is eager to please. This one says that reverse mortgages are risky business, and your company should be extremely careful:

> Therefore we recommend, for example, that a 95-year-old male living in a $300,000 home should get cash advances of $60 every month for as long as he lives in his home.

Wait a minute. That's only $720 per year! And this borrower isn't going to live a long time.

Who would sign up for such a small amount on such a valuable home? This "extremely careful" plan would be extremely *un*generous and even insulting to consumers. And it would be lousy public relations for any lender.

Of course the loan would not lose any money. The risk is so tiny that there would be no need to charge an insurance premium.

But you'd be embarrassed to offer this "extremely careful" loan. And even if you did, it wouldn't work. Consumer advocates would be all over you. And no one would take you up on such a bad deal.

Just Right: A Balancing Act

So what have you learned from your two hotshot consultants so far?

Two things:

✓ If you make the loan advances "too generous," that is, if you make them "too large," then the risk will be so great that it can't be shared among a group of borrowers.

✓ On the other hand, if you make the advances "too careful," that is, if you them too small, then the risk will be tiny. But the advances will be much "too *un*generous" for consumers.

In either case, you don't have a workable plan. But these extreme failures can help you find a more moderate plan that does work.

Somewhere A Place For Us

All you need to do is "find a happy medium" somewhere between "too generous" and "too careful." Finding the right balance between these two extremes is the solution to the reverse mortgage risk-sharing problem.

At various points toward the middle, there are specific plans that couple acceptable risk (and reasonable premiums) with acceptable loan advances.

Each risk-sharing lender finds a different point in this middle ground. But they all get there using the same general method. They estimate the amount of the losses they expect on a group or "pool" of loans. Then they calculate the premium needed to cover these losses.

You can see how this process works by imagining less extreme versions of the two consultant reports. As you make these plans less and less extreme, they begin to make more and more sense. Balancing "generousness" and "carefulness" is the key to reverse mortgage risk-sharing.

Rating the Risk

Fine-tuning a risk-sharing reverse mortgage involves analyzing the risk factors in detail. We won't do that now. But let's see what we can learn from a quick look at the general idea.

As you learned from the consultant reports, two key risk factors are the value of the home and the borrower's age.

For example, if two borrowers are the same age, you can make larger advances to the one with the more valuable home. If one home is worth $60,000 and the other is worth $300,000, then you can lend more to the owner of the higher-valued home without increasing your risk.

On the other hand, if two borrowers each own a $100,000 home, then you can lend more to whichever borrower is older. On average, the younger borrower will live longer. This means more monthly advances, and a longer time for interest to build up on the loan.

By contrast, the older borrower will most likely get fewer monthly advances over a shorter period of time. Therefore you can lend more per month without increasing your risk.

Some of the other factors that risk-sharing lenders must consider are the cost of the loan, and the long-term rate of appreciation on the homes in the risk pool. But that takes us much further than we need to go at this point.

In the next chapter, we introduce the basic types of reverse mortgages. Each handles the risk of loan loss in a different way. Some use risk reduction methods only. Others combine risk reduction with risk sharing.

Chapter 10

Reverse Mortgage Types

You wouldn't use a screwdriver to pound in a nail. But that's because you know

✓ there are different types of tools, and

✓ each tool is right for some jobs, but not others.

The same can be said of reverse mortgages. Before you can consider using them, you need to understand what the different types can and cannot do.

This chapter gives you a brief introduction to the main types of reverse mortgage loans. In Part FOUR, you will see the details of each type in depth. But for now, here is an overview.

Two Basic Types

The two main forms of reverse mortgages are

☐ *public sector* loans made by state and local government agencies; and

☐ *private sector* loans made by various mortgage lenders such as banks, credit unions, savings and loan associations, and mortgage banks.

Public Sector Loans

Public sector reverse mortgage programs generally came into being before private sector plans, and there have been more of them. For many consumers, a government loan plan has been the only one available. Most of the reverse mortgages written to date have been made in the public sector.

But these loan plans have definite limitations. Not everyone is eligible for them. Most often, they are available only to homeowners with low or moderate incomes. And they may not be available in all parts of a state or local government area.

The other major limitation is that the money you get from these programs usually can be used only for a specific purpose. In some programs, it must be used to make home repairs. In others, it can only be used to pay your property taxes.

Public programs may be limited in how you can use them (and, therefore, in the *amount* of money you can get). But they shine when it comes to paying the bill.

Simply put, public plans are generally much less costly than private sector plans. The loan fees and interest charges range from moderate to very low - or even "zero" in some programs. Because they are fairly simple programs with no risk sharing, public sector reverse mortgages do not charge insurance premiums.

Within the public sector category, two main kinds of programs are currently being offered:

◆ deferred payment loan programs for home repairs and improvements; and

◆ property tax "deferral" programs for paying your property taxes.

These programs are analyzed in Chapters 18-19.

Other types of programs have been developed by state housing finance agencies in Connecticut, Maryland, Montana, Rhode Island, and Virginia. These programs tested some of the loan features that were adopted later on in the private sector. At present, the Montana Board of Housing (406-444-3040) is the only agency offering its own reverse mortgage plan.

Private Sector Loans

Private sector reverse mortgages have taken a longer time to develop than public plans. But then they are more complex, and provide more benefits.

These loans are generally available to persons of all income levels. Your income doesn't have to be *above* a certain level - like it does in most private loans. On the other hand, it doesn't have to be *below* a certain level - like it does in public sector reverse mortgages.

The money you get from a private reverse mortgage can be used for any purpose. Moreover, there is a wide choice of loan advance types and amounts in these plans. And, in most cases, you can protect some of your equity for your heirs or for other future uses.

Simply put, you can generally get much more out of a private sector plan than a public one. But it will most likely cost you more - perhaps a lot more. The true, total cost of these loans is not as obvious as it might appear. But, in general, you pay a higher price for the greater benefits of a private plan.

Within the private sector, there are three different varieties of reverse mortgage:

♦ FHA-insured;

♦ lender-insured; and

♦ uninsured.

TABLE 5: Basic Types of Reverse Mortgages

LOAN TYPE	Limits on Borrow- er's Income?	Limits on Use of Loan Ad- vances?	Repay- ment Due on a Fixed Date?	Loan Costs at Market Rates or Below?
PUBLIC SECTOR	Yes	Yes	No	Below Market
PRIVATE SECTOR:				
Insured	No	No	No	Market
Uninsured	No	No	Yes	Market

Insured loans involve risk sharing as discussed in the last chapter. All of these loans (FHA-insured and lender-insured) include a premium charge, and require no repayment for as long as you live in your home.

Uninsured loans do not involve risk sharing. There is no premium, but you do have to pay back the loan

79

on a fixed - that is, a definite - date. These are the only reverse mortgages that do not put off repayment until you die, sell your home, or permanently move.

These private sector plans are analyzed in Chapters 20 through 24.

Beyond the Basics

So there you have it:

✓ You have now seen the basic definition and main features of reverse mortgages.

✓ You have watched the rising debt rise and the falling equity fall.

✓ You have learned about risk reduction and risk sharing.

✓ You've been formally introduced to the basic types of reverse mortgage loans.

Now you are ready to dig in. **Part THREE** takes a giant step beyond the basics. It shows you how to take apart and examine the inner workings of any reverse mortgage.

Take a break if you like. But then put on your apron. Roll up your sleeves. It's time to slice and dice.

Part
THREE

Analyzing Reverse Mortgages

Chapter 11

Three Little Questions

And now for the big question that's been nibbling at you: If a reverse mortgage were a machine, what would go in the top, and what would come out the bottom?

OK, so maybe it's *not* the issue you had in mind. And maybe **Figure 1** *doesn't* strike you as being very sophisticated. But together, they show you how the most basic financial features of any reverse mortgage can be uncovered by asking three little questions.

The Reverse Mortgage "Machine"

Forget about the technical details of reverse mortgages for a minute. Put aside *how* they work. Instead, think about *what* they do in general. What do you start out with? And what does a reverse mortgage *do* to it?

To make a reverse mortgage work, you need to have some equity in a home. That's the raw material, the "input." If a reverse mortgage were a machine like the one in **Figure 1**, home equity would go in the top.

Then you would turn the crank on the right side of the machine, and it would go to work. But what would it do with the home equity? What does a reverse mortgage turn home equity into?

Divided Into Three Parts

All of your home equity is divided into three parts by a reverse mortgage:

♦ *loan advances* that you get from the lender;

♦ *loan costs* that you pay to the lender; and

♦ *leftover equity*, if any, which goes to you or your heirs at the end of the loan.

At its simplest, a reverse mortgage is a "machine" for turning your equity into these three "products" or "outputs."

And, since that's what a reverse mortgage does, you can analyze any particular type or brand of reverse mortgage by asking these three questions:

✓ What do I get? (loan advances)

✓ What do I pay? (loan costs)

✓ What would I have left? (leftover equity)

At the end of any reverse mortgage, all of your equity will have been turned into one of these three products: loan advances, loan costs, or leftover equity. The basic question, of course, is *how much* of the equity will have gone into *which* of the three areas under any plan.

Figure 1: The Reverse Mortgage "Machine"

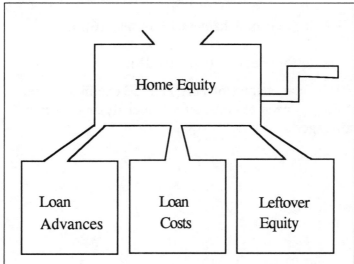

85

Three's a Must

Just remember this: you have to look at the answers to *all three* questions before you can see the full story. You can't focus on just the advances, just the cost, or just the leftover equity.

A great loan advance might mean higher costs but much less leftover equity. Two plans with the same loan advances might have quite different costs. If you want to see the big picture, you have to ask each of the three little questions.

In the next five chapters, you will learn more about the three "products" of the reverse mortgage machine:

◆ loan advances (Chapter 12),

◆ loan costs (Chapters 13-14 and 16), and

◆ leftover equity (Chapter 15).

The final chapter of Part THREE examines other issues you need to consider when analyzing reverse mortgages.

86

Chapter 12

What Do You Get?

An obvious first question to ask about any reverse mortgage is, "What's in it for me?".

There are two parts to this question: what *kind* of money can you get, and how *much* money can you get?

The *types* of loan advances differ from program to program. The *amounts* of money depend on which loan advances you choose, and other factors.

Loan Advance Types

As you have seen, public sector reverse mortgages are usually limited to one-time, lump sum advances (for home repairs), or annual advances (for paying property taxes).

Private sector plans, on the other hand, offer you more choices: lump sums, monthly advances, lines-of-credit, and combinations of these types of advances. Each loan advance type, or combination of types, is best suited for different purposes.

Lump Sum Advances

Most private sector plans offer some kind of "lump sum" advance at closing. In some cases, you can get this large, one-time advance only if you also sign up for a monthly advance as well. And in these cases, the amount of the lump sum may be too limited to meet your needs.

In other plans, you can put all of your available equity into a single lump sum of cash. Or you can split it between a lump sum at closing and an ongoing line-of-credit account.

Like It or Lump It

If you put all of your available equity into a lump sum, however, this doesn't mean you would be able to get an amount of cash anywhere near the amount of equity in your home. You wouldn't even be able to get as much as you could on a home equity loan.

Remember, the reverse mortgage lender is putting off all repayment for as long as you live in your home. This means your debt (lump sum plus interest) could keep increasing for a long time. So the lender has to leave "room to grow."

Monthly Advances

Most private sector plans offer one or both of the following monthly loan advance options:

☐ a *tenure* plan provides fixed monthly advances for as long as you live in your home, that is, for as long as you have "tenure" in your home;

☐ a *term* plan provides fixed monthly advances for a specific period of time, that is, a definite number of years or "term" that you select at closing.

Both plans provide a steady source of extra cash to you each month. It comes to you as a check in the mail, or it is directly deposited into your checking account. These plans are for people who are looking for more money on a regular, monthly basis.

Get Me A Tenure

In the tenure plan, you keep getting the monthly advances until you die, sell your home, or permanently move away. Even if you live to be 110? Yes. Even if your home decreases in value? Yes. Even if you live to age 110 in a depreciating home? Yes.

In the term plan, by contrast, the advances stop on a specific date. In most term plans, you do not have to repay the loan at this time.

The amount of the advance in the term plan, however, is usually greater than the advance in the tenure plan. And the shorter the term you choose, the larger the monthly advance will be.

In both plans, the amount of the monthly advance never changes. It is the same "fixed" amount every month. This means it's subject to inflation. You may like the look of an extra $350 a month now, but what will it buy ten, fifteen, or twenty years from now?

In some plans, you can prepare for inflation by putting some of your equity into a line-of-credit. This reduces the amount of your monthly advance. But it gives you a way to supplement it in the future.

Line-of-Credit Advances

A line-of-credit account or "creditline" lets you choose how much money to get, and when to get it. It turns your home equity into a personal account that you control.

It's sort of like a checking account. You decide how much money to use, and when to use it. The difference is that each "check" you write is a loan advance that creates debt against your home.

You can put all of your equity into a "standalone" line-of-credit. Or, you can add a smaller creditline to a monthly advance, a lump sum at closing, or both.

Another way to think of the creditline is as a *series* of lump sum advances that you control. You might use some of your line-of-credit next month, and then not use the account for another year or more. Later on, you might use it for an entirely different purpose.

Taking Your Lumps

Creditlines are well suited for the "what if's" of life. What if your roof doesn't last as long as you do? What if you need to purchase home care services? What if you need money for an emergency?

Line-of-credit advances can also be used to finance planned purchases. They have certain advantages over other types of debt. Because of that, you may even decide to finance some purchases for which you would otherwise use cash.

Just about anyone who is leaning toward a monthly advance should consider adding a line-of-credit. It does reduce the amount of the monthly advance. But it also gives you something to fall back on if you need to leave your home for health purposes, for example.

We are only beginning to see how useful reverse mortgage creditlines can be. In the first 500 federally-insured reverse mortgage loans, about two out of three borrowers included a line-of-credit in their plans.

As you will learn later on, however, you must carefully weigh the many benefits of a creditline against its cost. If a line-of-credit is little used, the cost can be very high.

Loan Advance Amounts

In most private reverse mortgages, you can choose the types of loan advances you want. You can also decide *how much* of your equity you want to get in each type of advance.

A Quick Example

If you are 75 years old and live in a debt-free home worth $100,000, you might be able to choose from among any of the following options:

☐ $350 per month for as long as you live in your home; or

☐ $800 per month for 5 years, $500/month for 10 years, or $400/month for 15 years; or

☐ a line-of-credit in the amount of $37,500 that grows by 10% each year; or

☐ $250 per month for as long as you live in your home plus a $10,000 line-of-credit that grows by 10% each year; or

☐ $300 per month for 15 years plus a $10,000 line-of-credit that grows by 10% each year; or

☐ a $10,000 lump sum at closing plus $230 per month for 10 years plus a $10,000 line-of-credit that grows by 10% each year.

These are just *some* of the choices you might have under the federally-insured reverse mortgage program. In fact, you can split up your equity among the different types of loan advances in any way you choose.

In other private plans, you can get larger advances than these. But you may find some limits on the amounts of equity that can be put into creditlines or paid out as lump sums at closing.

Keep in mind that no matter which plan you use, there is only so much equity in your home. The more types of advances you select, the more that equity will be split up into different parts. And the more you put into one area, the less will be left for the others.

Factors in the Mix

As you have just seen, the amount of money you can get from a reverse mortgage depends on how you decide to take it.

It also depends on

✓ *your age* (the older you are at closing, the more money you get),

✓ *your home's value* (the greater it is, the more money you get), and

✓ *your loan costs* (the smaller they are, the more money you get).

93

Age

Your age at closing is the one that counts. If you are married, some programs will use the age of the younger spouse. Others will "blend" your ages using actuarial (life expectancy) formulas. Joint borrowers who are not married are usually treated the same way.

Home Value

Some programs will make you a loan only if your home is worth more than a certain amount. Or only if the combination of your home's value and your age produce a loan advance of at least some minimum amount. Other programs limit the amount of home equity that can be put into their formulas for determining loan advance amounts.

You can boost the amount of your loan advances by completing major property repairs or improvements *before* closing your loan. If this increases the value of your home, you will be eligible for greater loan advances.

Loan Costs

The cost of the loan includes all fees, closing costs, insurance premiums, and the interest charged on the loan balance. That might sound fairly obvious. But the next two chapters show you it's not always as clear as it might first appear to be.

Chapter 13 looks at the costs you learn about at closing. But Chapter 14 shows you what you actually end up paying.

Chapter 13

What Does It Cost?

What you see is generally what you get when you look at the cost of *public sector* reverse mortgages.

Most often the only cost is the interest charged on the loan advances. And the rates are usually low to moderate.

If there is no interest charged, then the cost of the loan is especially easy to see - and take.

Private sector loans are a much different story, however. They have more different types of cost. And - most importantly - what you think you see is not always what you get.

The various loan costs you see at closing may be much higher - or much lower - than the real, total price you actually pay when the loan is over. We'll look at what you see in this chapter, and what you get in the next.

Into the Funhouse

In the private sector, it is natural to look at reverse mortgage costs in the same way as you look at for- ward mortgage costs.

But in many cases, that's like staring into one of those funhouse mirrors as if it were a real mirror. You think you've gotten taller and thinner. But in reality you haven't changed at all.

The method you normally use to evaluate the cost of a forward mortgage isn't *useless* when applied to reverse mortgages. It does provide vital information.

But if that's the *only* method you use for evaluating reverse mortgages, you can get a very distorted picture of the true cost of these loans.

That distortion could end up being very costly. You might think you understand the costs of one plan ver- sus another. But the reality could be quite different.

The Checklist Method

The traditional way of looking at loan costs is to make a list of cost categories at closing, and then fill in the blanks. If we apply this "checklist" approach to a reverse mortgage, we come up with the following:

✓ *origination fee* - to pay the lender for setting up or "originating" the loan; usually expressed as a percentage of the home's value or the amount of equity being mortgaged;

✓ *third-party costs* - to pay parties other than the lender for items such as an appraisal, title search and insurance, required inspections, recording fees, servicing fees, and the like;

✓ *insurance premium (or other risk-sharing fee)* - to cover the risk that the more flexible reverse mortgage programs with larger loan advances will have losses on some loans; usually expressed as a percentage of the home's value or the amount of equity being mortgaged;

✓ *interest charges* - to pay the cost of borrowing the loan advances; charged on the loan balance, and then added to the loan balance.

After making a list of the different cost categories, the next step in the checklist method is to find out what is being charged in each category. Here's where it starts to get murky.

Wavy Mirrors

Let's say the origination fee is 2.0%, the third-party costs are $1,100, the insurance premium is 3.0%, and the interest rate is 9.5%. How much does this loan really cost? Would it be a better deal if the premium were lower and the interest rate higher - or vice versa?

And how would you compare the overall cost of this loan to reverse mortgages with different ways of charging risk-sharing premiums? For example

☐ a "split" premium: 2.0% at closing, plus 0.5% added to the interest rate;

☐ a premium determined directly by the amount of appreciation in the home's value over the life of the loan;

☐ a premium that purchases a deferred annuity in your name;

☐ variations and combinations of the above.

Is it getting murky yet? Or can you guess which is the best deal? In fact, any plan you select would be the wrong answer. The only correct answer would be "none of the above."

That's right. Not one of these private sector plans would *always* be the best deal. Different plans would be the best deal in different situations.

The main problem with the checklist method of comparing loan costs is that it doesn't tell you this. It doesn't give you a hint that each loan plan has an overall cost pattern that differs from that of other plans.

Checklist Problems

Looking at loan costs one part at a time helps you see each part at closing. But it isn't the best way to see the *total* cost you actually pay when the loan is done.

In particular, the checklist approach doesn't take into account three basic reverse mortgage features: cost financing, cost limits, and risk sharing.

Three Blind Spots

In a forward mortgage you are concerned about the loan costs at closing because they take cash out of your pocket at that time. In a reverse mortgage, you can finance these costs (that is, add them to the loan balance and pay them back when the loan is over).

This doesn't take cash out of your pocket now, and in some cases it could even save you money in the long run. It all depends on how long you live in your home, and what happens to its value.

In a forward mortgage, it is unlikely that the loan balance will ever exceed the home's value. But in a risk-sharing reverse mortgage, the lender *expects* to have some loan losses. That's why an insurance premium is charged - to cover the losses. When do these losses occur? It all depends on how long you live in your home, and what happens to its value.

Risk-sharing reverse mortgages are unlike forward mortgages in a third way. Some reverse mortgage borrowers using the very same plan end up paying much less for their money than others do. It all depends on how long you live in your home, and what happens to its value.

Hear an echo? A lot sure seems to depend on how long you live in your home and what happens to its value. If we set them to music, those words would be the theme song of these chapters on loan costs.

Chapter 14 explains these long-term cost patterns in detail. Before doing that, let's sum up the main problem with the traditional way of looking at loan costs.

Current Charges v. Long-Term Costs

The checklist method keeps you from seeing the long-term cost patterns on risk-sharing loans.

It tends to focus your attention on the *individual amounts charged* to your loan balance at closing rather than the *total rate actually paid* when the loan is over.

In short, the checklist approach looks at a reverse mortgage as if it were a forward mortgage. Funhouse mirrors are fun, but you really need to see the full and true picture when your home equity is at stake.

Chapter 14

What Do You Pay?

The true, total cost of any risk-sharing reverse mortgage can vary tremendously.

At the extremes, the cost can end up being very high or very low. You can't tell for certain what the real cost will be when you first sign up for the loan.

Because these types of loans involve risk sharing, some borrowers will pay much more - or much less - than others for the very same loan.

Unknowns in the Mist

Everything you know at loan closing will probably have much less to do with the overall cost of the loan than two things you can't know for certain:

♦ how long you will live in your home, and

♦ what will happen to its value.

If the interest rate on the loan is adjustable (that is, if it is subject to change over the life of the loan), then future interest rate adjustments become a third "unknowable" factor in overall loan costs.

The pattern of loan advances can also affect the cost of the loan. That's the one factor you have some control over, although you may not know at closing just how you will actually end up using a line-of-credit, for example.

The "Total Loan Cost" Method

So how can you evaluate the cost of a reverse mortgage with all these "unknowables"? And how can you do so in a simple way that makes it easy to compare loans with different cost factors?

The answer is to combine *all* the cost factors - including the non-recourse limit - into a single average annual rate: the Total Loan Cost (TLC). To do this, you need to make assumptions about what might happen in the future. In other words, you figure out what the TLC rate would be *if* the loan runs 15 years and your home appreciates at 4% per year. Then you figure it out at different times and appreciation rates.

You keep on doing this, and pretty soon you can see the loan's overall cost pattern. Each loan has its own pattern of TLC rates, although the rates for loans in any one program will tend to be similar.

Technically, the TLC is the annual average interest rate that would produce the total amount owed at any point during the loan if it had been charged on the loan advances made prior to that point.

Put simply, it's the single rate that includes all the loan costs. It gives you a simple way of comparing the cost of different loan programs. It shows you how - and how much - the cost of these loans can vary based primarily on how long you live in your home, and how much your home's value changes.

Figuring the TLC

Lenders in the federal reverse mortgage insurance program are required to figure out TLC rates for you. You can ask other lenders to show you how TLC rates on their loans compare.

But it's important to have a general sense of where these numbers come from. If you do, it will be easier to make sense of them. So here's a quick look at how you figure out the TLC rates on any reverse mortgage:

1) make an assumption about how long you will live in your home (loan term) and what will happen to its value (appreciation rate);

2) figure out - or ask the lender - the total amount you would owe at that point;

3) enter this information and your loan advances into a financial calculator;

4) solve for the interest rate (see Appendix A for more detailed instructions);

5) repeat steps 1-4 using a variety of loan terms and appreciation rates.

Did you notice that in step 2 we combined *all* of the cost factors on the loan? The total amount you would owe at some future time is determined by using all of the cost factors from the checklist approach. In addition, step 2 includes a factor that the checklist method leaves out: the non-recourse limit on the loan.

In one sense, you really don't care about the particular details of *how* the total amount owed is determined. You only need to know *how much* you would owe at some future time.

Then you ask the financial calculator, "What single rate of interest charged on all the loan advances over the term of the loan would produce the *total* amount owed at the end of the term?" This method lets you combine all the factors into one rate.

If you follow the steps outlined above on a sample reverse mortgage, you would end up with something like **Table 6**. This table shows the TLC rates on a specific loan at various points in the future at three different rates of appreciation: 0%, 4%, and 8%.

The loan is a federally-insured mortgage providing about $350 per month at 10% interest to a 75-year-old borrower for as long as she lives in her home, which is worth $100,000 at closing. The loan includes no lump sum at closing, and no line-of-credit.

To simplify things even more, the interest and appreciation rates are assumed to be fixed. That is not likely to happen in fact. But for any given pattern of rate changes, there is a comparable fixed rate. The fixed rates used to calculate the TLC, therefore, also represent a variety of adjustable rate patterns.

Analyzing the TLC

So what do you learn about the true cost of risk-sharing reverse mortgages from this table? They are

◆ expensive in the short run,

◆ less costly over time, and

◆ moderate to inexpensive if you live longer than average in a home that appreciates at a moderate to low rate.

Table 6: Total Loan Cost (TLC) Rates

	When home value grows at . . .		
	0%	4%	8%
TLC rate after . . .			
2 years	48.4%	48.4%	48.4%
7 years	14.8%	14.8%	14.8%
12 years	10.3%	12.3%	12.3%
17 years	3.7%	10.3%	11.5%
22 years	0.7%	6.1%	11.2%

That's the overall pattern you will see on all risk-sharing reverse mortgages providing monthly loan advances. Let's look at it more closely.

Expensive Early On

As you can see, the TLC rates are the greatest in the earliest years of the loan. And that's no funhouse mirror. The total annual average rate after two years *is* 48.4% at all appreciation assumptions.

But what does that mean? If the individual cost factors are roughly the same as they are on an insured forward mortgage (and they are), then why is the early TLC rate on a reverse mortgage so high?

The answer is that TLC rates include *all* the loan costs together. *AND,* in this reverse mortgage, you are getting your money one month at a time, instead of all at once like you do on a forward mortgage.

When you get the full amount of the loan at closing on a forward mortgage, the start-up costs (origination fee, third-party costs, insurance premiums) are a much smaller part of the overall amount owed at that time. As a result, the TLC rate would be much smaller.

But when you get only part of the cash (in this case just $350) each month on a reverse mortgage, the start-up costs are a much larger part of the overall amount owed in the early years of the loan. As a result, the early TLC rate is much larger.

Coverage Not Needed

In another sense, the loan is so costly in the short run because you paid for a long-term guarantee that you ended up not needing. You paid for the security of a monthly payment for as long as you live in your home, and then you only lived there a short time.

It's sort of like paying auto and fire insurance premiums all your life, and then never having an accident or a fire. In each case you get the coverage, but it turns out you didn't need it.

Less Costly Over Time

Table 6 also shows you that the Total Loan Cost comes down over time at all appreciation rates.

This happens because the start-up costs become a smaller part of the overall debt as more advances and interest are added to the loan balance. So the longer you live in your home, the lower the TLC rate becomes.

Notice also that the TLC rate comes down the fastest when the appreciation rate is the lowest - and vice versa. For example, at the end of year 17, the rate is 10.3% at 4% appreciation. But at lower appreciation (0%) the TLC is lower (3.7%). And at greater appreciation (8%), the TLC rate is greater (11.5%).

The appreciation rate is important because it determines how much your home is worth. And that has a direct bearing on cost because of the non-recourse limit. (Remember? You can never owe more than what your home is worth.)

If your home does not grow in value, for example, then your rising loan balance would be much more likely to reach the value of your home. And, once it does, your debt is limited by that value. At greater rates of appreciation, it becomes less likely that your debt will rise enough to catch up to your home value.

Least Costly Later

Did you also see in **Table 6** that the *real, total* cost of the loan can actually become **less** than its stated cost at closing?

Check this out. The total start-up costs on this loan are $4,000 (1% origination, 2% "upfront" insurance, and $1,000 in third-party payments). In addition, the interest rate charged on the loan balance is 10.5% (10.0% plus a 0.5% "periodic" insurance premium).

Now, when you combine the 4% start-up costs with the 10.5% ongoing interest charge, you would expect to get a total interest rate greater than 10.5%. And you do - in some cases. But you don't - in others.

Less Than You Thought

For example, if your loan runs 17 years and your home appreciates at 4% per year, the Total Loan Cost rate is 10.3%. If the loan runs longer or if the growth rate is lower, then the TLC rate is lower still.

In all of these cases, the real cost of your loan ends up being less than it looked like it would be at closing. That's because you live in your home longer than average and your home's value increases at a moderate to low rate.

This means that your loan balance grows to reach the value of your home. Once that happens, your debt is controlled by the non-recourse limit. As a result, the real rate on your loan drops beneath the stated cost, and then it keeps on dropping over time.

Put another way, if you live longer than average you may not have to pay any of the start-up costs, and your real interest rate may be less than the stated rate you signed up for.

Your below-market cost of debt is made possible by the insurance premiums paid by all the borrowers

☐ who left their homes before their rising loan balances reached their home values, or

☐ whose home values grew at above-average rates of appreciation.

109

But you can end up "finessing" (that is, not paying) the start-up costs only if you financed them. If you paid them in cash at closing, then that money is gone and the potential for a bargain TLC rate is reduced. You may end up paying for something that you otherwise would have gotten at no cost.

An Average Annual Rate

Keep in mind that TLC rates are *average* annual rates. For example, the TLC rate on a reverse mortgage might be 15% at the end of the ninth year, and 9% at the end of the fifteenth year.

This does *not* mean that the rate is 15% *during* the ninth year, and 9% *during* the fifteenth year. Instead, it means that the annual rate over the first nine years *averages 15% per year*. But if the loan runs fifteen years, then the overall average annual rate drops to 9%.

In other words, the longer the loan runs, the lower the average annual TLC rate will be over the full length of the loan.

Learning From The TLC

TLC rates help you see that the cost of a risk-sharing reverse mortgage is a moving target. Your natural tendency is to assume that the costs you are given at closing (start-up costs plus interest rate) are the costs on the loan. You assume that what you see is what you get.

But TLC rates show that the real pattern of total costs over time involves a wide range of possibilities. These costs could be much higher or much lower than what you might have expected at closing.

Understanding TLC rates is an important part of understanding reverse mortgages. At the very least, it can keep you from misusing these loans. But there are limits to the TLC concept, too.

Not For Short Times' Sake

Perhaps the most obvious lesson to be learned is that reverse mortgages can be very expensive in the short term. So, for example, you should think twice before signing up for a monthly advance for as long as you live in your home if you intend or expect to live in your home only for a short time.

Such a loan would be *very expensive* on a Total Loan Cost basis. An uninsured reverse mortgage, if available, would be a much less costly choice in this situation. And an insured loan with monthly advances for a fixed term would provide greater advances.

Spend to Save?

If you wanted to reduce your TLC rates in the early years of your loan, you might be tempted to take all your money in a lump sum at closing. Or to spend more of a creditline sooner than you otherwise might.

It's true, of course, that both of these actions would reduce the early TLC rates on your loan. They would

111

do so by making your start-up costs a smaller part of your overall debt in the early years of the loan.

But that doesn't mean either of these would be smart financial moves. Much would depend on what you used the money for.

Investing? Refinancing? Spending?

You might be thinking of investing a large lump sum to produce monthly income. But if you invest safely, the interest rate you earn no doubt would be much less than the interest rate you would be paying on your loan.

That's a formula for losing money. If you used this approach instead of taking a monthly advance, you would probably get less cash per month, or have a less secure source of cash - or both.

Some people use a reverse mortgage to pay off another debt. This gets them out from under a monthly repayment requirement. And it frees up the income they had been using to make those repayments. Like any other swapping of old debt for new, however, you need to look at the numbers.

What's the interest rate on the old debt versus the new debt? What does it cost to set up the loan? How much extra cash will this refinancing get you each month? How long do you expect to remain in your home?

If you have a creditline, you would get your money at a better overall rate if you took more of it out sooner. But then you would have less money left later.

112

Should you be so intent on getting a good rate that you spend your money less carefully than you otherwise might? Being "rate wise, but spending foolish" doesn't make a lot of sense.

Hope for the Worst?

TLC rates are great for showing you the basic cost patterns in these loans. But that doesn't mean you should do *everything* you can to get the lowest rate possible. A lower TLC rate could even be something you might choose to avoid!

Consider the case of the TLC Grinch. This creature appeared to a prospective borrower one day. It looked into the future, and announced that the consumer's home would appreciate at 4% per year forever.

But then it gave the borrower a one-time opportunity to change this annual rate to either 0% or 8%. It pulled out a copy of Table 6, and showed the borrower that a 0% appreciation rate would mean a much lower TLC rate, and strongly recommended the 0% rate. The consumer liked the idea of getting the lowest overall rate. Everyone knows that a lower interest rate is better than a higher interest rate.

Pinch the Grinch

What's wrong with this picture? Think about where the low rate comes from in this case. It's based on no appreciation. That means much less - or no - leftover equity later. So choosing the lowest real rate might mean having no money left at the end of the loan.

113

What else would it mean? On a forward mortgage, getting a better rate means having smaller payments to make. So on a reverse mortgage, you might expect a better TLC rate would mean greater loan advances paid to you.

But in this case it doesn't. The loan has already been closed. What happens to the value of your home after that point does not change the loan advances.

So the net result is that getting a lower TLC rate *through a lower appreciation rate* would be against your best interests. Yes, the lender would end up with more money if there's more appreciation. But so would you! And you wouldn't lose anything.

You would clearly be better off turning down the TLC Grinch's first recommendation. Yes, you would like the lower TLC rates. But tell it you'd prefer getting them by living in your home longer than average. Oh, and you'll take the 8% appreciation rate, too.

TLC Rates in Focus

Your little run-in with the TLC Grinch helps put these rates in the proper context. They are helpful in understanding the true, total cost of risk-sharing reverse mortgages. But they are only projections.

In other words, you can't know for certain what the rates will be when your loan is closed. You can only tell what they will be *if* you live in your home a certain length of time and *if* your home's value grows at a certain rate. That's because the true, total cost of your loan depends mainly on those unknowable factors.

So comparing the cost of one program versus another involves comparing their overall TLC rate *patterns*. One loan may be the better deal than another in the short term, but not in the long term. One loan's TLC rates may be affected by appreciation rates much more than another's.

Comparing TLC rate patterns shows you how costs compare over time and at different appreciation rates.

Finessing the Premium

With the TLC approach, you evaluate a reverse mortgage more like you would an insurance policy, an annuity, or some other risk-sharing product. The difference is that you probably won't be paying much if anything in cash when you close a reverse mortgage.

Although you obligate yourself (or your estate) to pay for the loan in cash at a later time, neither you nor the lender know at closing how much it is going to cost. In fact, you probably could not even come very close in estimating how much your loan will end up costing.

The main reason for this is that you are buying more than an individual loan. You are also buying into a risk-sharing "pool" that makes these kind of mortgages possible. And, as with any risk-sharing product, you may or may not end up getting financial benefits from the premium charged to your loan.

If you do get financial benefits, you get them in the form of a low TLC rate. In effect, you may get the benefits without ever actually paying the premium. If you live in your home longer than average and your home's value increases at a moderate to low rate, you stand a good chance of finessing (that is, not paying) the premium and other start-up costs.

On the other hand, if you live in your home a shorter than average time, then you most likely would not get financial benefits. You would end up actually paying the premium, and your overall TLC rate may be very high.

And Now, A Short Cut Method

Now that you've seen the shortcomings of the traditional checklist method; now that you've endured the ins and outs of TLC rates; now that you've had just about all you can take; *now* we show you a simple short-cut method for evaluating loan costs on a reverse mortgage.

No, you haven't learned more than you need to know about these costs. It's just that once you've seen the details, it's easier to take a step back and use a handier, simpler approach.

It's waiting for you - in Chapter 15.

Chapter 15

What's Left Over?

How important is leftover equity?

If you live in your home for the rest of your life, then your loan would be repaid by your estate after your death.

Do you want any persons or organizations to inherit some of your equity? If not, then the amount of leftover equity might be of little concern to you.

But what if you do not live in your home that long?

What If You Move?

All of us no doubt would strongly prefer living in our own homes for the balance of our days. But not all of us will be able to do so.

What would happen if you permanently moved away from your home during your lifetime? In that case, your loan would become due and payable. And that most often means selling your home.

The amount of equity left over after paying off the loan would be yours. But would it be enough? How much equity would you need? What would you do if there were very little or no equity left?

The amount of equity left at the end of the loan will depend largely on your home's value at that time. If your rising loan balance has caught up with that value, then you would have no equity left. But if the value of your home is greater than your loan balance, then you would get the difference.

Projecting the Net

You can't know for certain if or exactly when you might move in the future.

And - unless you've got better sources than the rest of us - you can't know for certain what the value of your home might be at that time. So you can't know for certain just how much equity you would have left.

118

But you can figure out how much you would have left *if* you move out after a certain number of years, and *if* your home's value grows at a certain rate between now and then. In other words, you can project what your leftover equity would be based on different assumptions about the future.

If you make enough different assumptions, you will see an overall pattern of leftover equity under each plan, somewhat like the TLC rate table in Chapter 14.

This information can help you choose between one plan and another. It can also help you make decisions about how much of your equity to put into the different types of loan advances.

It might even convince you to consider preserving some of your equity.

Just In Case You Move

There are two basic ways of planning for the possibility that you may move in the future.

One way is to take out a line-of-credit, and then be sure not to use it all up. Whatever you don't use will then be available to take out just before you move.

That will work if you can keep your hands off of the amount you've decided to save. So perhaps you'd like to keep that money at a safer distance, making it more difficult for you to get at. If so, then you should consider the other way of planning for a move.

Preserving Equity

An important optional feature available in most private sector plans is *equity preservation*.

This option is especially well suited for setting aside equity for heirs, other bequests, and burial expenses. Unlike a line-of-credit, it ensures that equity will be available after your death. A creditline is for your personal use only. It cannot be used by others.

Equity preservation lets you divide your equity between loan advances and leftover equity. You do this at loan closing by setting aside a fixed amount or percentage of your equity in a reserve account.

Playing Keep Away

A fixed *amount* of preserved equity is protected by the loan's non-recourse limit. In other words, you can never owe more than the value of your home *MINUS* the fixed amount. The fixed equity reserve account becomes the final loan advance made by the lender to you or your estate at the end of the loan.

A fixed *percentage* of preserved equity means that the amount left over in the future will depend on appreciation - or depreciation.

If your home is worth $100,000 and you preserve 20% of its value, you would have $20,000 in your reserve account at closing. At the end of the loan, you would get the $20,000 *PLUS* all the appreciation on that amount. Or, for example, if your home *depreciated* by 10%, you would get a check for $18,000.

With a fixed amount of preserved equity, the amount never changes. With a fixed percentage, the amount could grow substantially as you home appreciates. Or it could decrease if your home depreciates.

Playing Hard To Get

Depending on the specific details of any plan, you might also be able to use equity preservation as a kind of hard-to-get-at cash reserve *during* your loan.

A lender may let you use your preserved equity as security for a loan from a different lender. Or it may let you turn some of that equity into loan advances at a future time. In either case, the procedure wouldn't be as quick and easy as getting a creditline advance. And there probably would be substantial additional costs.

But this approach might give you the protections of an equity reserve account plus some of the flexibility of a creditline. You may or may not be able to get another loan or to refinance, however. And the added cost might be greater than you are willing to pay.

Putting Up Equity Preserves

Keep in mind that the more equity you preserve at closing, the less will be available at that time to put into loan advances.

Remember the reverse mortgage "machine"? There are only three things that can happen to the equity you start out with. It can be turned into loan advances, loan costs, or leftover equity. That simple fact brings us to the easiest and most direct way of evaluating reverse mortgage costs.

121

The Short-Cut Cost Method

Isn't it about time for a formula? Cover up the rest of the page, and see if you can make any sense of this:

$$HE = LA + LC + LE$$

Here's a hint. HE stands for "home equity," and LA stands for "loan advances." That's it, you've got it. It's the reverse mortgage machine expressed as a formula:

Home Equity = Loan Advances

+ Loan Costs

+ Leftover Equity

Now rearrange the factors to show what "loan costs" equal:

$$LC = HE - (LA + LE)$$

You can use this formula to compare the cost of different reverse mortgage programs. Here's how it's done.

Apples With Apples

Let's say you're talking to two lenders offering similar reverse mortgages. Both claim that their plan is the better deal financially.

They can't both be right. But it's hard for you to tell from the information they give you. One plan has greater advances, but the other would leave you more equity in the future. Which is the better deal?

You get the answer by comparing apples to apples. In other words, you tell each lender you need to see how much equity you would have left in the future if you got exactly the same loan advances from each lender.

Remember, you are the one who decides how much of your equity should go into which types of loan advances. Give the same plan to each lender. Tell them both, for example, that you want $300 per month for as long as you live in your home.

Ask them to show you how much equity you would have left at various points in the future at various appreciation rates. Ask each lender to use the same advances, loan terms, and appreciation rates.

Most Leftover = Least Costly

Then you just look to see which loan leaves you the most equity. If both provide the same advances, then the one that leaves the most equity costs the least.

It's only common sense. It comes straight out of the loan cost formula we figured out on the last page:

$$LC = HE - (LA + LE).$$

If two loans have the same HE (the equity in your home) and the same LA (the loan advances you selected), then you can just strip those factors out of the formula. The result is this simplified version:

Loan Costs = Leftover Equity.

That's the short-cut method of looking at reverse mortgage costs. But it only works if both of the loan examples being compared have the same home equity, loan advances, loan terms, and appreciation rates.

One advantage of this method over the TLC approach is that it keeps us safe from the TLC Grinch - the imp that would have us sacrifice leftover equity for lower TLC rates. On the other hand, the short-cut method makes it difficult to see how the real cost of a single loan changes over time.

When you compare two loans using the short-cut approach, however, the relative cost patterns are easy to see. And - as with TLC patterns - it is clear that no reverse mortgage program always provides the lowest loan cost.

One plan will be the best deal in some cases, but not others. It all depends on how long you live in your home, and what happens to its value.

The next chapter looks at these two key factors - life expectancy and home appreciation - in greater depth. In Part FIVE, we will use the short-cut method to compare different reverse mortgage programs.

Chapter 16

Handicapping the Cost

Remember "The Price Is Right"?

The TV game show where you had to guess how much things cost?

Good thing that was before reverse mortgages.

Can you imagine a contestant saying "It depends"? Can you imagine the emcee saying "That's right!"?

It would be strange, all right. But the answer would be correct, if incomplete. As you have learned, the cost of most private sector reverse mortgages does depend on these two major factors:

✓ how long you live in your home, and

✓ what happens to its value.

And, as you have also learned, loan costs affect the amount of equity you would have left at the end of the loan.

Get Out Your Crystal

At closing, neither you nor the lender can know for certain what your loan will end up costing.

Will you live in your home for a short time, a long time, or just about average? Will your home's value increase at a high rate, a low rate, or just about average?

Do you have any idea at all? Actually, you are probably better able to make a stab at answering these questions than the lender is.

The lender doesn't know about your personal health situation, or how long your parents lived. The lender may also not have as long or detailed a knowledge of home value changes in your neighborhood as you do.

Although no one can know the answers in advance, you can learn more about the questions. And this will make the information you already have more useful.

Range on the Home & Life

Our purpose here is not to guess the *exact amount* of your loan costs. Instead, it is to estimate the *general range* within which you expect your loan term and appreciation rate to fall.

In other words, you make you best guess about how long you expect to live in your home. At least how many years? But probably not longer than how many years? What is the short and the long of it most likely to be?

Then you do the same for your appreciation rate. What are the lowest and highest rates most likely to be on your home?

With these overall ranges in hand, you can learn more from the TLC rate tables and leftover equity tables in later chapters. This approach will help you get a general idea as to what your loan will cost, and how much you will have left over when it is done.

And it will give you a way to compare different loan programs. Remember, each will be the better deal in some cases but not others. By figuring out your most likely cost range, you will be able to see which loan is most likely to be the better deal for you.

Learning a few things about life expectancy and appreciation rates doesn't mean you will make a better guess about what your loan costs will be. But it might mean you will be less apt to make an extremely bad guess.

With that rousing introduction, let's take a look at these two key cost factors: home appreciation and life expectancy.

Whither Real Estate?

"No one knows."

It's tempting to stop right there. About the only clear improvement you can make on that statement is to add the phrase, "Many predict, but . . . "

Inflation As A Guide?

Historically, home values have risen at a somewhat higher rate than consumer prices in general. But no one knows if that will continue in the future.

Some are predicting it won't because of the "birth dearth," that is, the fact that there will be relatively fewer people of first-home-buying ages during the 1990s.

But others say that would only lead to less home-building, which would tend to keep home values growing. They also predict that many baby-boomers who did not buy homes in the 1980s will be starting families and becoming homeowners in the 1990s.

So take your pick: the traditional view that home values rise faster than inflation, the doomsday view of values falling behind the inflation rate, or the middle-of-the-road view that home prices will grow at a rate roughly equal to the general rate of inflation.

Whichever you select, you still don't know what the general inflation rate will be. And even if you did, that's a national average. Housing market conditions in your region, area, and neighborhood may be quite different from national trends.

National Averages

In putting together the federal reverse mortgage insurance program, the U. S. Department of Housing and Urban Development used a long-term, nationwide annual average home appreciation assumption of 4%.

At the same time, the Social Security Trustees Annual Report was projecting a long-term consumer inflation rate (Consumer Price Index) of 4% per year.

Four per cent is quite a bit lower than the 7% to 8% national average growth rates for home values during most of the 1970s and 1980s. But then it's hard to find anyone who expects to see those rates in the 1990s. So 4% seems like a reasonably conservative guess at this time.

To cover a range of possibilities, the tables in this book show three different rates: 0%, 4%, and 8%.

Local Realities

But what about *your* home? How has its value changed?

The best guide is homes like yours that have been sold in your neighborhood. You can't predict what will happen in the future by looking at the past. But you can get a general sense of how volatile or how stable these home values have been.

Have you seen a lot of big price increases for a long time followed by more recent decreases? Have values been increasing slowly but steadily? Has there been little change in prices for a long time?

Four per cent may be as reasonable a long-term national *average* appreciation projection as any other. But clearly, annual changes in the value of any *single* home can easily be greater than 8% or less than 0%.

Ain't Speculatin'

So what are you doing speculating in real estate values? That's the question some reverse mortgage borrowers have asked themselves.

Any owner of property bears the risk of appreciation. Will the property grow in value or not? How much will it grow? Could you get a better or safer return on your equity elsewhere?

A risk-sharing reverse mortgage lets you turn some of this risk over to the lender. This may appeal to you if you expect little appreciation on your home - or if you don't want the value of all your equity dependent on the volatility of local housing markets.

But then the smartest move will turn out to have depended on what happens to the value of your home. And as you've seen, we didn't add much - if anything - to that "no one knows" statement a few pages back.

Let's see if we can do better with the other major factor in most reverse mortgage loan costs: how long your loan runs.

How Long Will This Be Goin' On?

"How long you live in your home" includes

☐ *how long* you live, and

☐ *where* you live.

This Is Your Life Expectancy

How long will you live? No one knows for certain. But your best guess will probably be based on both personal information and statistical trends.

You do know some things that may affect how long you will live: your personal health history, your current health status, and how long your parents and grandparents lived.

These factors could tell you whether or not you are likely to live as long - or longer than - other persons of your age and sex. But how long do persons of your age and sex live?

Take Thee To An Actuary

There are different types of life expectancy tables. If you use the wrong one, it could lead you astray.

For example, you might have read recently that the life expectancy of Americans is about 75 years. Does this mean that a 65-year-old has on average about ten years to live? No, it does not.

It means that the average number of years of life *counting from birth* is 75. In other words, it tells you how long newborn babies will live on average.

The average number of years of remaining life *counting from a certain age* - for example, from age 65 - is a different matter. This is a more select group. It does not include all those persons who died before that age. In other words, these are survivors - people more likely to live longer than the 75 year average.

These survivors didn't die in infancy. They made it through their teenage years, young adulthood, and middle age. All the people who did die at these earlier ages are included in figuring out the 75 year average life expectancy of all persons counting from birth.

But when you figure out remaining years of life counting from a certain age, you don't include all the people who died before that age. You are only inter-ested in how much longer the survivors will live.

132

Table 7 shows life expectancy figures counting from various ages. For example, a 65-year-old female has on average another 18.4 years to live.

This does not mean, of course, that every 65-year-old female will live exactly that long. In fact, most will live a longer or shorter time. But the average for all female 65-year-olds will be about 18.4 years. Put another way, if you make it to age 65, the odds are that you will live to be 83.

Table 7: Average Remaining Years of Life from Various Ages

AGE	Male	Female		AGE	Male	Female
65	14.2	18.4		78	7.6	9.8
66	13.6	17.7		79	7.2	9.2
67	13.0	17.0		80	6.8	8.7
68	12.5	16.3		81	6.4	8.2
69	11.9	15.5		82	6.1	7.7
70	11.4	14.8		83	5.8	7.2
71	10.8	14.2		84	5.4	6.8
72	10.3	13.5		85	5.1	6.4
73	9.8	12.8		86	4.9	6.0
74	9.4	12.2		87	4.6	5.6
75	8.9	11.6		88	4.3	5.3
76	8.5	11.0		89	4.1	5.0
77	8.0	10.4		90	3.9	4.7

Source: National Center for Health Statistics: U.S. Decennial Life Tables for 1979-81

Annuitants Anomalous

Don't be surprised if you run into a table that is like Table 7 except for this: all the numbers are larger.

In fact, probably most of the life tables you see do have longer life expectancies than the ones in Table 7. The reason is that these tables are even more exclusive. They only include persons who buy annuities. And those people live longer than the rest of us.

An annuity is a guaranteed monthly income that you purchase from a life insurance company. There are many variations on this general theme. But the basic idea is that you pay a lump sum of cash to buy the annuity, and then the insurance company sends you a check every month for as long as you live.

In other words, the company takes on the life expectancy risk. The longer you live, the more checks you get, and the better deal you get - and vice versa.

Longer Than Average

As you might guess, the companies keep a close watch on how long their annuitants live. And they have learned that people who buy these risk-sharing annuities tend to live longer than average. In short, they tend to attract people who have reason to believe they might live longer than normal.

That's one reason why "annuity mortality" tables have larger numbers than Table 7, which includes *all* persons who have lived to various ages. The other reason is that the annuitant tables also include some amount of profit for the insurance companies.

Will the life expectancies of reverse mortgage borrowers be more like that of the general population, or more like that of annuitants?

Both products involve risk-sharing that provides greater benefits to persons who live longer. But you need to pay for an annuity with cash, whereas the start-up costs on a reverse mortgage can be financed.

Offsetting Corrections

It's probably safe to say that the life expectancies of reverse mortgage borrowers will fall somewhere between the figures for the total population and the figures for annuitants only. So the numbers in Table 7 may be somewhat *lower* than they should be.

But the goal here is to estimate the length of the loan *term*. So you have to consider that some borrowers will not live *in their homes* for as long as they live.

In this sense, the numbers in Table 7 are *greater* than they should be. We'll explore why that is so in the next section. The more important point for now is that this fact gives us offsetting corrections to Table 7.

In other words, the figures are too low because they have no "annuitant bias." On the other hand, they are too high because they have no "move-out" bias.

If you were designing a reverse mortgage insurance plan, you would have to make precise estimates of each bias. For our purposes, that kind of gory detail might only give us a false sense of precision.

A Moving Experience?

What are the odds that you would move out of your home after taking out a reverse mortgage?

Again, not an easy question. Statistics on how often people move at various ages aren't very helpful. They include all people who move for any reason.

Reverse mortgage borrowers are a more select group. In general, they have stronger ties to their homes and neighborhoods. Getting the cash needed to remain in their homes may have been a key factor in taking out a reverse mortgage in the first place.

Financially, moving can be very costly to reverse mortgage borrowers. If you do so, your loan becomes due and payable. This means that any monthly advances you are receiving will stop.

If you have lived past your life expectancy, there is a good chance that your rising debt has reached your home's value. The only equity you would have left if you were to move would be whatever you might still have left in a line-of-credit or in a reserve account.

Shorter Than Average

So in addition to wanting to stay in your home, you may have a strong financial incentive to do so. As a group, that makes you and other reverse mortgage borrowers unlike the overall population of people your age. In other words, you would be less likely to move than other people your age.

But there will be *some* moving done by reverse mortgage borrowers during their lifetimes. As a result, the average term of risk-sharing reverse mortgages is no doubt *less* than the life expectancy of reverse mortgage borrowers.

"Cost" as a Handicap?

Back in Chapter 11, you learned the three little questions that unlock the financial details of reverse mortgages. Then you worked your way through each of the three basic products of these loans.

En route, you learned that the real cost cannot be known at closing. And it can end up being very high or very low.

Now you know that it is very difficult even to make a rough estimate of the costs. About all you can do is

✓ understand the general pattern of costs relating to loan term and home appreciation;

✓ make your best guess about the general ranges within which your loan term and appreciation rate are most likely to fall; and

✓ using these ranges, compare the projected costs of different reverse mortgage programs.

Facing the Unknown, Again

But how much sense does it make to analyze costs in such detail when all you can do is guess?

Clearly, it is very important that you understand the basic pattern of reverse mortgage costs. An educated guess is much better than being totally ignorant or seriously misinformed about costs. But it doesn't give you the kind of hard information and precision you would like to have.

In one sense, that's because you are dealing with the very same kinds of uncertainties you have in so many other areas:

- ☐ Should you use your savings, or cut down on expenses?

- ☐ How much of your savings should you use?

- ☐ How long will your savings last under different circumstances?

- ☐ Should you take that pension as a lump sum or a monthly payment?

- ☐ As a monthly payment for life, or for a fixed term of years? Based on one life or two?

The "iffy-ness" of reverse mortgage costs is not unlike these types of uncertainties. And, as you have seen, reverse mortgage costs can vary tremendously - from *very* expensive to below-market "bargains."

What Are You Buying?

If it's impossible to get a firm fix on what you pay, maybe you need to concentrate more on what you get.

After all, even if you *could* know the cost of these loans in advance, would it be perfectly obvious what a reasonable price would be?

Remember, risk-sharing reverse mortgages aren't just loans. They are loans with annuity-like income guarantees. They cover the combination of mortality risk and appreciation risk. In other words, the risks that you will live so long or your home will appreciate so little that you loan balance will reach the value of your home.

Within certain limits, you select the types and amounts of the loan advances. You also designate any equity to be preserved. This package of benefits gives you a certain measure of financial security, flexibility, and independence. There may be no other way to get the combination of benefits that a reverse mortgage provides.

Take a Hard Look

Take a hard look at what you get. Think about what it would mean to you. Of course it would be nice to have more money. But what would you use it for?

How important would the goods and services you buy be in your life? How much difference would they make?

Then take a hard look at the range of possible costs and leftover equity. Remember, whatever you use now, you won't have later. On the other hand, perhaps the time has come to start using the equity in your home.

Now, weigh the benefits and what they would mean to you against the possible costs. Seem worth it to you? How does it compare with other options (see Chapter 26)? That's what it all comes down to. And only you can decide if the benefits outweigh the costs.

That's as far as we'll take it for now. In Part THREE you have learned what to look for in analyzing reverse mortgages. Upcoming in Part FOUR, you will consider all of these issues with respect to specific programs.

But first let's take a quick look at some of the things you should look *out* for.

Chapter 17

On The Lookout

"Whadaya get? Whadaya pay? Whadaya left over?"

These three technical topics cover the general financial issues involved in reverse mortgage borrowing. But there are other questions you need to consider as well. Some of them are obvious, others aren't.

In this chapter we look at the following issues: availability, eligibility, appraisals, debt limits, repayment requirements, lender default, and disclosures.

If Not Now, When?

Reverse mortgages are still in an early stage of growth. Availability at present remains spotty. And legal issues are still a problem in a few states.

A constitutional ban on many types of debt in Texas is the most serious barrier to reverse mortgage lending. But a test case could clear up the matter. Some plans face less serious obstacles in New York and Massachusetts, where corrective legislation has been introduced (see **Resources**).

The good news is that new forces are afoot to help you find and effectively demand reverse mortgages. In Part FOUR, you will learn about the current availability of each program in detail. You will also learn a seven-step plan to get lenders to start new programs.

Tell Them What You Want

Consumer demand has always played a key role in reverse mortgage development. Of late, an array of new services to lenders has made this type of lending much easier than ever before. A consumer armed with this knowledge can be very persuasive in getting lenders to start a program. More on this in Chapter 23.

In general, it is also a good strategy to contact multi-state lenders that are not yet offering their reverse mortgage programs in your state. By contacting them now and getting on their waiting lists, you will be encouraging them to expand into your state.

Eligible for What?

Each program really has two sets of rules for deciding who's eligible for a reverse mortgage: the official ones, and the practical ones.

Officially Yours

The official rules are easy:

✓ you have to own a home,

✓ there's usually a minimum age, and

✓ often there's a limit on the amount of current debt against your home.

All programs provide loans on single family detached homes. But not all of them accept duplexes, 3+ units, condominiums, planned unit developments, or cooperatives.

If it's a public program, you probably must have an income that is not greater than a certain amount. There may also be a limit on the value of your home.

In some private programs, there is a limit on the amount of equity that can be used to figure out your loan advances. In others, there may be a home value minimum, or a requirement that your age and home value generate a monthly advance of at least a certain amount.

Unofficially Not Yours

If you are just a bit over a program's age minimum, you are officially eligible for the program.

But you may be eligible for such small loan advances that as a practical matter, it doesn't make any sense. If you are married or if your home's value is low, this can make the situation even worse.

So you can be officially eligible, but unofficially "too young" to get the amount of money you need. Remember, the younger you are, the smaller your advances because your life expectancy is longer.

If you are in your sixties, your reaction to this may be to forget about reverse mortgages altogether. But the real lesson is that you should take out no reverse mortgage before it's time.

But Maybe Someday

It's no accident that the typical reverse mortgage borrower to date has been a 75-year-old single person. She gets more out of it than a 65-year-old couple.

But a 65-year-old couple can take this into account in planning for the future. They can count on getting greater advances in the future for two or three reasons:

☐ they will be older,

☐ their home will probably be worth more, and

☐ one of them may become widowed.

144

In the Eye of Whom?

How much is your home worth today?

The answer is a major factor in determining the amount of your loan advances - and some of your start-up costs. The higher the value, the greater your loan advances - and the greater your start-up costs.

A private lender will arrange a professional appraisal to determine your home's current value. But you need to keep an eye on this.

Does the price seem reasonable to you? If it does not, ask the lender to explain it to you, or have the appraiser explain it. If you aren't familiar with real estate dealings, ask someone who is to listen to the explanation.

Remember, you are no doubt paying for this service, and the appraisal - once accepted by you - will determine much of the financial shape of your loan.

If the price still seems wrong, you might ask for a second opinion by another appraiser. You may even want to hire one yourself. In either case, it might help you negotiate a better price.

Getting A Good Price

Although you are not moving out, and you are not giving up ownership, taking out a reverse mortgage is something like selling your home in this way: it means coming up with a price for your home.

When you cash in on one of your most important investments, you want to get a good price for it. And when cashing in takes the form of a reverse mortgage, that means bird-dogging the appraisal.

No More Than What?

The non-recourse limit is a key part of any reverse mortgage. It keeps your debt from ever being greater than the value of your home.

But there are different ways of making this limit work. In some loans, the limit is defined as the "net sale proceeds," that is, the amount of money left after your home is sold.

This means that the cost of selling your home (for example, a realtor's commission or fee) comes from the sale proceeds. Neither you nor your estate would be responsible for the cost of selling your home.

In other plans, the non-recourse limit is defined as a percentage of your home's sale price. For example, one program limits your debt to 93% of the amount paid by the new owner.

This means that if you sell your home yourself, you get to keep 7% of its value. If you pay a realtor 5%, you get to keep the other 2%. The same would be true for your estate.

Be sure to read the non-recourse section of your reverse mortgage documents carefully.

Say When?

Perhaps the most important "fine print" details in any reverse mortgage agreement are the acceleration and default triggers. No, these legal clauses have nothing to do with starting cars or earthquakes. But they could get you moving when you don't want to.

Every loan includes conditions that would require you to repay the mortgage. The general ones are

- ◆ when you die (or when your surviving spouse or other co-borrower dies),

- ◆ when you sell your home, or

- ◆ when you permanently move away.

But of course it's not as simple as that. The loan documents define these conditions in detail. They also spell out other conditions that

- ◆ would cause you to be "in default" on your loan, and

- ◆ could "accelerate" your loan repayment.

In other words, these conditions would permit the lender to make your loan due and payable. This would probably mean selling your home and moving. So you need to be certain that you understand these details completely. Be sure to go over them carefully until you do.

De Fault of De Borrower

Many of the default clauses are exactly the same ones you find on a standard forward mortgage:

✓ failure to pay property taxes

✓ failure to maintain and repair the property

✓ failure to keep the property insured.

The mortgage gives you certain rights to "cure" or take care of any default. It also lets the lender make additional advances to cover these expenses if necessary. Be sure you understand

1) the procedure for "curing" any default;

2) the procedure the lender must follow in making advances to cover these expenses; and

3) the impact of these advances on your loan.

Other common default conditions you should look for and make sure you understand include

✓ personal bankruptcy

✓ donation or abandonment of the property

✓ fraud or misrepresentation by the borrower

✓ eminent domain or condemnation proceedings.

Pedal to the Metal?

Reverse mortgages also include some unique conditions that cause your loan repayment requirement to be "accelerated" or speeded up. In other words, to make your loan due and payable sooner.

These acceleration clauses usually cover changes in your situation that affect the security of the loan. They might include

✓ leasing or sub-letting all or part of your home (check to see what the mortgage permits);

✓ remarriage (will a new spouse be an owner of the property and get survivorship benefits?);

✓ new liens (will new debt be permitted if it is made secondary to all reverse mortgage debt?).

Be sure you understand the details of every condition that accelerates the loan. But be especially careful when you read the loan's definition of a "permanent" move.

What Does "Permanent" Mean?

Reverse mortgages must be paid back when you permanently move away from your home. But what does that mean exactly?

What if you leave your home for a month? For six months? A year? Can you take a long vacation? What if you have an operation, and then need to recuperate someplace other than your home?

What if you become seriously ill, leave your home for health reasons, and then don't know whether or not you will be returning to your home? What happens then?

In general, the mortgage will permit you to be away from your home for any reason up to a certain length of time. But then it may require that you get the lender's prior written approval to be away for any longer period of time.

An overall limit of one year is typical. In other words, if you do not live in your home for one year, the lender could make the loan due and payable.

If you are gone for a long period of time, the mortgage may require that you take steps approved by the lender to protect the property in your absence. This could mean getting someone to live in it, take care of it, or check on it from time to time.

What Now, My Lender?

What happens to your loan if something happens to your lender? You take out a reverse mortgage for the financial security, flexibility, and independence it provides. But what kind of problems do you have if your lender has problems?

Reverse mortgage loan advances become a key part of your retirement income plan. What do you do if your lender is unable to continue making them? What happens if the *lender* defaults on your loan?

De Fault of De Lender

Your loan documents should spell out exactly what your rights are if the lender fails to make a loan advance.

The documents should specify

✓ how you should inform the lender that an advance has been late or missed;

✓ how the lender must respond to avoid being in default;

✓ what you must do if the lender does not respond as required; and,

✓ most importantly, the penalties the lender must pay for late advances and for defaulting on the loan.

For your protection, the penalties should be so strong that it would be financially foolish for a lender to be late or to default. In one plan, late advances are subject to a 10% penalty. In another, defaulting lenders lose *all* interest on the loan.

Remember, you will be counting on those loan advances. The very best time to watch out for your future rights is well before you sign any documents.

Of course, if you take a federally-insured reverse mortgage, the federal government will step in and continue the advances for any defaulting lender.

151

T-I-L There Was You

The federal Truth-in-Lending (T-I-L) Act requires that lenders give you the details about the costs and terms of your loan in writing before closing. The T-I-L Act also gives you three business days after closing to cancel the deal. If you change your mind for any reason, you must tell the lender *in writing* before the three days are over.

Sweating the Details

As you can see, there are many details involved in any reverse mortgage loan. In general, public sector programs are the simplest and easiest to understand. In the private sector, all federally-insured loans have to include certain legal protections prescribed by federal law. Other private loans can be more complicated and vary quite a bit.

Whichever type of program you select, you need to understand all the parts of your loan documents. That's why it's a good idea to have someone other than the lender look at the legal papers with you.

In **Part FOUR**, you will learn about the specific costs, benefits and other features of currently available reverse mortgages in greater detail. It begins with the public programs (deferred payment loans, property tax deferral), and then covers the private plans (uninsured, FHA-insured, and lender-insured reverse mortgages).

152

Part
FOUR

Reverse Mortgage Programs

Chapter 18

Deferred Payment Loans

The simplest reverse mortgage is the deferred payment loan for home repairs and improvements.

This public sector loan is usually offered by a local government agency. It can be quite limited in terms of how much money you can get, and what you can do with it.

But it can also be an excellent value *if* you can find one, *if* you are eligible, and *if* it fits your needs.

What Do You Get?

A deferred payment loan gives you a one-time lump sum of cash. After you get this single advance at closing, you cannot get any more money from this type of loan. But no repayment is due until you die, sell, or permanently move.

The cash you get must be used to repair or improve your home. Each program has its own rules that define exactly what you can and cannot use the money for.

Permission Granted?

In general, these types of loans can only be used to fix a problem with your home, or make it a better place for you to live in.

Most often, the repair or improvement must make your home safer or sounder, or work better. In some programs, you can use the loan to make your home more energy efficient, easier to get into and around in, or easier for you to operate.

You generally can't use these loans to make your home simply *look* better, unless that is the result of some other work.

Most programs permit replacing or repairing

✓ floors,

✓ stairs,

✓ porches,

✓ roofs,

✓ wiring,

✓ plumbing, and

✓ heating equipment.

Some programs also permit the installation of

✓ ramps,

✓ rails,

✓ grab bars,

✓ storm windows,

✓ insulation, and

✓ weatherstripping.

Still other programs allow more ambitious accessibility improvements, such as widening hallways and doorways, or repositioning walls and doors.

In addition to the limits on the *use* of these loans, there are also usually limits on the loan *amount*. And, as a general rule, the amounts available in these public programs are much smaller than the lump sums you can get from private programs.

What of the Future?

Once you use a deferred payment loan, you are not able to get any more money from it. This debt against your property might also keep you from qualifying for any other type of loan against your equity.

Let's say you take out a deferred payment loan today, and then try to take out a private sector reverse mortgage at some later date. The new lender probably would require you to pay off your deferred payment loan with a lump sum from the new loan at closing.

If the new loan could not provide a large enough lump sum, you might not be able to get the loan at all.

Willing To Take Second?

On the other hand, the new lender may agree to make you a reverse mortgage *without* requiring that you pay off the deferred payment loan. This probably would happen only if the public lender agreed to take a secondary position to the private loan.

In other words, the private lender would be first in line to get paid back at the end of the loan. The public lender could only be repaid after the private loan is fully repaid.

Many public sector lenders *are* willing to do this. The main reason they make these loans is to help keep up the housing stock. They want to prevent declining property values and neighborhood deterioration. These goals are met even by loans that are not fully repaid.

Public-Private Partnerships

Some public lenders are even willing to take a secondary position from the very beginning of a loan. The *combination* of a private sector reverse mortgage with a public sector deferred payment loan can be a good deal for everyone.

The public agency gets an improvement in the housing stock. The private lender gets better collateral for the loan (a repaired or improved home), and the borrower gets lower overall loan costs.

So even if your needs are greater than a deferred payment loan alone can meet, it's worth your while to look into them. They just might meet part of your needs at a *very* reasonable cost. And the rest can be covered with cash or a private loan.

What Do You Pay?

There are serious limitations to what you can get from a deferred payment loan. But what you pay is generally not a problem.

Each program has its own costs. But usually they are low or less than low. Most often there are no origination fees, no third-party costs, and no insurance premiums. Like it so far? There's more.

In some programs, the interest rate is zero per cent. In other words, there is no interest. You just pay back the amount you borrowed. These are examples of reverse mortgages that are *not* rising debt loans.

In the programs that do charge interest, it is typically very low to moderate: roughly 2% to 6%. Sometimes the amount of interest depends on your income. The lower your income, the less interest you pay.

To Forgive, Divine

In some programs, there is even a partial or total forgiveness of the lump sum advance! This is usually determined by how long you live in your home.

For example, if you borrow $10,000, you might get your debt reduced by $1,000 for every year after closing that you live in your home. If you live there for ten years, you would owe nothing.

In another program, you may owe the full amount until a certain point is reached, and then owe nothing.

TLC Not Needed

No matter how you measure it, the cost of most deferred payment loans is very low. So low, in fact, that you don't need to calculate the Total Loan Cost (TLC) rates that are so important for understanding most private sector reverse mortgages.

Due to the general absence of start-up costs, TLC rates are basically the same as the stated interest rate on deferred payment loans. And that rate is usually so low that it is obviously a good deal.

Looking in the Mouth

Deferred payment loans are probably the most attractive loans you'll ever see. But that doesn't mean you should run right out and get one. Open those jaws. Take a good look at that horse's teeth.

✓ Do you really need to make that repair or improvement?

✓ What will it actually mean to you and the quality of your daily life?

✓ How long do you expect to live in your home?

✓ Does the program let you make the repair or improvement you need and want?

✓ Will the program take a secondary position behind another loan at closing? In the future?

✓ If you would like your heirs to live in your home, does the program permit them to pay off the loan on a monthly basis? At what rate?

If a program in your area charges no interest and forgives the loan advances over time, it would be especially hard to resist. If you expect to live in your home until the debt is erased, you would actually come out ahead.

But that's not the only way this could happen.

What's Left Over?

In most deferred payment loans, there's a lot of leftover equity. That happens because

☐ the amount of your single loan advance is somewhat limited to begin with,

☐ the start-up costs are minimal or non-existent,

☐ the interest rate is low or non-existent, and

☐ in some cases, the principal advances are forgiven partially or totally.

Put all that together and it spells "a lot of leftover equity."

So much, in fact, that you could actually make money on the deal. This is not something you can count on. It's not a reason for taking out the loan. It may not happen all that often. But it is not "pie in the sky" either.

More Than You Started With?

Let's look at an example to see what would have to happen for you to come out ahead.

Assume your home is worth $75,000, and you borrow $10,000 for a major improvement. Assume also that the interest rate is zero, and your home will appreciate at 4% per year.

Now comes the iffy part. Many home improvements increase the value of your home. Some more than others. Some might even decrease the value.

But since we're assuming here, let's say you make the type of improvement that gives your equity a solid lift. It makes your home much more attractive, and substantially increases the amount someone would be willing to pay for it. This usually means a kitchen make-over or a bathroom re-do.

And, since we're in charge of the assumptions here, we'll say your $10,000 investment increases your home's value by about 70% of the loan amount, or $7,000. That's a lot, but neither unreasonable nor unheard of. Now let's see how it plays out.

Pays Its Own Way

Table 8 shows what would happen to your home's value if you do, and do not, take out the loan described above. Then it compares the results.

Table 8: Deferred Payment Loan; Impact on Home Value*

HOME VALUE	At Closing	After 5 Years	After 10 Years
Without loan	$75,000	$91,249	$111,018
With loan	$82,000	$99,766	$121,380
Difference	$7,000	$8,517	$10,362

* See "More Than You Started With?" starting on page 162.

As you can see, the improvement increases the value of your home by $7,000 right away. Then, that new value increases by 4% per year. At the end of ten years, the home is worth $10,362 more than if you had not taken out the loan.

In other words, you can use the increase in value to pay off the $10,000, zero-interest loan - and still have some left over. If the loan is a "forgivable" one, then you would get the full increase in value.

But Not Always

On the other hand, if the loan has an interest rate of 6%, for example, your debt would be nearly $18,000 after ten years. But the increase in the value of your home would pay off more than half of it. That's like getting a new kitchen at less than half price.

Of course, not all repairs and improvements would increase the value of a home by 70% of the loan amount, as we assumed in Table 8. And, not all homes will appreciate by 4% per year.

Maybe the added value will be more modest, and the appreciation slim. But even then it's hard to beat a deferred payment loan if you have an improvement or a repair you really need to make.

By now you are probably wondering

✓ How do you find and qualify for these loans?

✓ What can you do if they are not available in your area?

By Whom? For Whom?

The trickiest thing about finding deferred payment loans is that they often aren't *called* deferred payment loans. They go by various names. So you have to ask for what you want - "a home repair loan with no repayment till you die, sell, or move."

You can track these loans down by contacting the types of local government agencies that usually offer them or know where they are offered:

♦ city or county housing department

♦ area agency on aging or county office on aging

♦ community action agency

♦ community development agency

♦ senior citizen center

♦ neighborhood housing services agency.

If an agency you call does not offer these types of loans, ask what kind they do offer. And ask what other agencies might offer deferred payment loans.

In some states, the company that provides your gas or electricity also may provide deferred payment loans for weatherizing your home. Contact the company's consumer affairs department.

But Do You Qualify?

Once you find a deferred payment loan program, you can find out if you are eligible for a loan.

In most programs, that will mean your income must be below a certain level. Often there is also a limit on the value of things you own (assets). Sometimes your age must be greater than some minimum.

These loans are almost always permitted on single-family, detached homes. The eligibility of duplexes, 3+ units, and other types of dwellings varies with each program.

Your home will generally qualify for a loan only if its value is below a certain amount, or if it is located in a certain area. There may even be a limit on the amount of debt you can have on your home.

A Loan Program Deferred?

Can't find a deferred payment loan program in your area? Think there should be one?

It's an easy program for local governments to start up and operate. It helps keep up the tax base, so it can be a good investment of public funds. It's cheaper to run that an outright grant program. Many local agencies have made it a key part of their housing policy.

So talk to your city or county representatives. Encourage them to look into it. Excellent materials are available for justifying, designing, and operating these programs (see **Resources**).

Chapter 19

Property Tax Deferral

You could think of it as a new way to pay your property taxes.

Instead of paying cash now, you borrow against your equity. Later - when you die, sell, or move - the debt is repaid from the sale of your home. This lets you be a fully paid-up taxpayer now. But it also lets you defer - or put off - your actual cash payment until you actually cash in on your home's equity. Until then, you get to use the money.

What Do You Get?

Property tax deferral programs are public sector reverse mortgages. They let you take one loan advance each year for the purpose of paying property taxes.

Once you sign up for the program, you can decide whether or not you want to defer your taxes each year. Some programs will automatically defer the taxes unless you ask them not to. Other programs will defer the taxes each year only if you request them to do so. In either case, you make the decision.

The annual amount of your loan advance for any year cannot be greater than the amount of your annual property tax bill. These taxes usually run somewhere between 1% and 3% of your home's value.

Program Limits

Some of the programs have annual loan advance limits that may be *less* than your annual tax bill. This means you might not get enough money to pay your taxes in full.

Some programs also limit the total amount you can borrow over the life of your loan. This is usually a limit on the total loan balance as a percentage of your home's value.

In other words, if your debt reaches an amount that equals a certain portion of your home value, then you would not be able to defer any more taxes.

168

How Does It Work?

Each program is different. Some are run by state government agencies, others by local government offices. The rules vary from program to program.

Some require that you apply for deferral before you pay your taxes. If it is a state-run program, then the state government may send a check directly to the local government office that collects your taxes. Or it may send a check to you that is made out jointly to your local tax collector and you.

In other programs, you can apply after paying your taxes. Then you get a check made out just to you.

Many local programs don't bother with a check. They simply mark your tax bill "paid." That saves paperwork, but it's still a loan - and that means a lien.

Lien on You

Tax deferral programs generally place a lien against your property. This is a legal notice that does not permit the home to be sold or the title to be transferred unless the loan is repaid.

But a tax deferral lien is *not* the same as a "tax lien." A tax lien is placed on the property of owners who do not pay their taxes. But if you defer your taxes, you are *not* delinquent in paying them.

In fact you *have* paid them, with a government-sponsored tax deferral loan. You remain a fully paid-up taxpayer and are not delinquent in any way.

Closing Off Future Options?

A tax deferral loan is like a deferred payment loan in that it limits what you can use the money for. And these limits on loan uses also become limits on loan amounts.

That's fine if your needs are limited to these purposes. But you should also consider that these loans might keep you from qualifying for less limited programs in the future.

If you try to take out a private sector reverse mortgage at some later date, for example, the new lender would almost certainly require that your tax deferral lien be paid off with a lump sum from the new loan at closing.

And - especially if you have been deferring taxes for many years at a moderate interest rate - the new loan may not provide a large enough lump sum to pay off the deferral debt. As a result, you might not be able to qualify for the new loan.

Second to None

"But," you ask, remembering our discussion from the last chapter, "what about the tax deferral taking a secondary position behind the private loan?"

Not very likely without an equity reserve account.

The risk of loss is much greater on a tax deferral in secondary position than on a deferred payment loan. The total of all tax deferral advances can be much greater, and the interest rate is usually higher.

What Do You Pay?

More than on a deferred payment loan, but less than you end up paying on most private loans.

Property tax deferral programs generally do not charge an origination fee or an insurance premium. And most often there are no third-party costs.

The interest rate on the loan advances is usually fixed, that is, it does not change over the life of the loan. Although the rates vary, most of the state-run programs charge either 6% or 8% interest.

Keep It Simple!

In some cases the interest is charged on a "simple" rather than a "compound" basis. This can save you a lot of money, and make tax deferral a much better deal - especially if your loan runs a long time.

"Simple" means that interest is charged only on the amount of your loan advances. "Compound" means that additional interest is charged on the interest that has been added to your loan balance in the past, but not yet paid by you.

In other words, when the lender charges interest to your loan but doesn't require you to pay it, the lender is in effect giving you a loan advance to "pay" the interest (that is, letting you finance the interest). This loan advance is then subject to interest charges just like all other loan advances.

171

Paying compound "interest on interest" means you are paying interest on the loan advances you were given to "pay off" past interest charges. Paying simple interest, by contrast, means the lender is *not* charging interest on the loan advances used to pay off past interest charges.

The dramatic difference between these two ways of charging interest is discussed in detail in the "What's Left Over?" section of this chapter. For the moment, think about the effect of simple interest charges on a tax deferral's TLC rates.

Less Than Meets The Eye

Like a deferred payment loan, there are few if any start-up costs on a property tax deferral loan. This means that the TLC rates on tax deferral are basically the same as a program's stated interest rate - with one glaring exception.

TLC rates are based on the assumption that a lender is charging interest on a compound basis. In the private sector, this is a safe assumption. It is only in the public or nonprofit sector that simple interest charges are sometimes seen.

If interest is charged on a simple basis, the TLC will be *less* than the stated rate on the loan. The longer the loan runs, the greater the difference between the TLC rate on a simple tax deferral and a compound tax deferral would become. Over a long period of time, the difference could be very large.

What's Left Over?

Unlike some deferred payment loans, tax deferrals *are* rising debt loans.

If you defer your taxes every year, then the total amount of your loan advances is growing. If your taxes are increasing, then you loan balance is growing even faster. And if the interest on your loan is charged on a compound basis, then it is growing faster still.

But, on the other hand, you have few if any start-up costs. And the annual amount of you tax bill is generally a small percentage of your home's value - usually somewhere between 1% and 3%.

Checking the Numbers

Table 9 shows what would happen on a tax deferral loan based on the following assumptions:

☐ home value at closing = $75,000

☐ annual increase in home value = 4%

☐ annual tax bill = 2% of home value

☐ interest rate on tax deferral = 6% compound; and 6% simple

☐ amount and frequency of deferrals = full tax bill every year

Table 9: Property Tax Deferral; Impact on Equity

		Compound Interest		Simple Interest	
End Yr	Home Value @ 4%	Loan Balance @ 6%	Leftover Equity	Loan Balance @ 6%	Leftover Equity
0	$75,000	$1,500	$75,000	$1,500	$75,000
5	91,249	11,490	79,759	10,437	80,812
10	111,018	26,913	84,105	21,310	89,708
15	135,071	50,053	85,018	34,539	100,532
20	164,334	84,060	80,275	50,634	113,700

At 6% *compound* interest, you would owe $11,490 after five years. But your home would have grown (at 4% appreciation) to a value of $91,249. So your remaining equity would be $79,759.

On the other hand, if 6% interest were charged on a *simple* basis, your debt would be $10,437. And your leftover equity would be $80,812.

Reading down Table 9, you see that the difference between compound and simple interest gets greater over time. That's because the compounding of interest "on interest" has a longer time to work.

After 20 years, your leftover equity would be much greater with simple interest - $33,425 greater! That's a pretty strong financial argument for simple interest tax deferral, wouldn't you say?

174

Compounding versus Inflating

But what if the interest is compounded - as it is in virtually all private sector loans - and your home appreciates more than the 4% rate assumed in Table 9?

If you had an 8% annual increase, for example, you would have plenty of leftover equity. It might not be as much as you think, however.

Remember, we are assuming that your annual tax bill equals 2% of your home's value. So if your home appreciates a lot, guess what happens to your taxes? And that increases your loan balance.

Here is how much equity you would have left if your home appreciated at 8% per year:

☐ after 5 years: $97,573

☐ after 10 years: $129,419

☐ after 15 years: $171,493

☐ after 20 years: $227,002.

Strong appreciation is clearly the key to leftover equity. Even with higher taxes. The greater the growth rate, the more equity you have left.

Limping versus Leaping

But what if your home doesn't perform this well? What if it chugs along at a very low growth rate, or doesn't grow at all?

If the $75,000 home in Table 9 did not increase in value, it would remain at $75,000 for every year of tax deferral. Not too promising, eh?

But wait a minute. We assumed that taxes would always equal 2% of home value. So if your value doesn't grow, your taxes don't grow - at least in our example. And that means you loan balance doesn't grow as fast.

Here is how much equity you would have left if your home did not grow in value:

☐ after 5 years: $64,537

☐ after 10 years: $52,543

☐ after 15 years: $36,491

☐ after 20 years: $15,011.

Perhaps it's a bit pessimistic to assume *no* appreciation over two decades. That would mean a decline in your home's real value, considering inflation.

But clearly it is possible. And if it did happen, you might run into a serious problem, depending on the details of your tax deferral program.

Hitting the Limit?

Some programs place a limit on the total amount of debt you can accumulate. If the limit is 80% of the home's value, then you would reach it after 20 years in the zero-growth example above.

176

At that point you would owe about $60,000 on a $75,000 home. If the program had an 80% debt limit, you would no longer be able to defer your taxes.

Of course, your taxes would be much lower in real (adjusted for inflation) terms. But you probably would be better off at this point if you had taken out a private, risk-sharing reverse mortgage providing monthly loan advances for as long as you live in your home.

The private loan might have been a better choice in this case because

✓ your total loan advances over the past 20 years would have been greater; and

✓ you would continue getting monthly loan advances for as long as you live in your home.

By Whom? For Whom?

Finding out if there is a property tax deferral program in your area is pretty simple.

You just contact the local government office where you pay your property taxes. They can usually tell you if there is such a program for homeowners in your state or community.

In a few states (see **Table 10**), a state government agency runs a program with the same rules all over the state. In these states, you can sometimes contact a local agency *or* a state agency for more information.

Table 10: State-Operated Property Tax Deferral Programs

STATE	CONTACT
California	State Controller's Office 1-800-952-5661
Illinois	County Treasurer's Office
Maine	Local Assessor's Office, or Maine Property Tax Division 1-207-289-2011
Oregon	County Assessor's Office
Washington	County Assessor's Office
Wisconsin	WI Department of Revenue 1-608-266-1961 (forms) 1-608-266-1983 (information)

In other states, the program may be set up by state law, but run by local governments. In some of these states, local governments can decide what the program's rules will be. In other states, they can decide whether or not they will offer the program to their taxpayers.

Local programs are available in all or parts of Colorado, Connecticut, Florida, Georgia, Massachusetts, New Hampshire, Texas, Utah, and Virginia. If you live in one of these states, contact your local tax collector for further details.

(In Iowa, there is a program for SSI recipients only. Applications are sent to eligible persons. Contact the Iowa Department of Human Services for information on Iowa Code 427.9.)

But Do You Qualify?

To be eligible for property tax deferral, you usually have to be aged 65 or over. In some cases the minimum age is lower, or there isn't one.

Most of these programs also have a limit on how much income you can earn. In the state-run programs, the maximum ranges from $14,000 to $32,000. But some programs do not have an income limit.

And, as you might expect, there is often a limit on the amount of any outstanding (unpaid) debt against your home. If you still owe quite a bit on your mortgage, or on a second mortgage or home equity loan, for example, you may not be eligible for tax deferral.

Chapter 20

Uninsured Private Programs

Public sector lenders don't have to be very worried about loan losses because their loans aren't very risky.

Deferred payment loans provide limited, one-time advances at low interest rates. Property tax deferrals provide small annual advances at moderate rates with an overall limit on loan balances.

In either case, there is little risk of loan loss for the lender. Put another way, a loan that provides limited benefits to consumers involves little risk for lenders.

But now we turn to private sector loans that provide greater benefits to borrowers. A little more difficult to figure out, but not impossible.

Mission: Not Impossible

Your assignment, should you choose to accept it, is to design a reverse mortgage that

✓ provides greater benefits for the consumer than public sector plans; but

✓ provides solid protection against loan losses for lenders.

You begin, no doubt, by consulting the consultant reports you had commissioned back in Chapter 9 when you used to be an insurance executive.

You conclude quickly, however, that this risk-sharing business with insurance premiums is just too complicated for the small bank you now work for. Besides, you are not certain you would do enough of these reverse mortgages to spread out the risks across a large enough group.

You decide to follow the "KISS" principle - "Keep It Simple, Stupid!". So you add a third element to the two-part mission statement above:

✓ *without* using any insurance premiums or any other risk-sharing methods.

Now your revised mission is to design a loan that delivers more benefits than public plans, but is less complicated than private, risk-sharing plans.

The only way you can do this is to use risk reduction methods. So you get out your financial calculator and you start pushing buttons. Not much later, you unveil the uninsured, private sector reverse mortgage.

Limiting the Loan Term

The key feature of this loan is that it must be repaid on a specific date. This is the only reverse mortgage that could require repayment *before* you die, sell, or permanently move.

If the repayment date occurs before any of these events, then the loan is due and payable on that date. If any of these events occur before the repayment date, then the loan is due and payable when any of the events occur.

You select the repayment date at closing. Then you get a monthly advance until you die, sell, or move, or until the repayment date - whichever comes first.

Limiting the loan term means that much of the risk of this reverse mortgage remains with the borrower. It is the borrower, after all, who takes the chance that the loan may come due before she is ready to sell and move. Can you imagine being forced to sell your home and move to repay a loan?

Of course, the lender is taking a big risk, too. If the repayment date is reached, and the borrower refuses to sell and move, what's a lender to do?

Take the ever-growing loan losses that can come with letting the debt grow? Or face the public relations nightmare of foreclosing on an elderly person who only wants to hold on to her home?

So there are serious problems with this type of reverse mortgage from both the borrower's and the lender's points of view. Is it any wonder that so few of them exist?

Yet these uninsured private sector loans can be an excellent value in the right situation. And they do a good job of showing us the practical limitations of a simple reverse mortgage without risk sharing.

What Do You Get?

In most of these programs, the amount of your monthly loan advance is determined by

✓ the value of your home;

✓ the loan term, that is, the length of time between closing and the repayment date;

✓ the interest rate; and

✓ the "loan-to-value" limit.

For example, let's say you select a 5-year term and the interest rate is 10%. Your monthly loan advance would be the amount that would grow to reach the "loan-to-value" limit on the repayment date.

The "loan-to-value" limit is the largest balance the lender will permit on the repayment date - expressed as a percent of your home's value at closing. Assume the limit is 80% and your home is worth $100,000 at closing. This means your monthly advance is the amount that will grow to reach $80,000 in five years if 10% interest is charged on the advances.

To keep it simple, let's say you pay start-up costs in cash instead of financing them with the loan. In this case, your monthly advance would be $1,024.56. You would get that amount every month for five years - and then you would have to pay back $80,000.

Loan Limits Reduce Risk

The loan-to-value limit and the definite repayment date protect the lender. If the limit is 80%, for example, then the loan balance at the repayment date cannot be greater than 80% of the home's value at closing.

So even if the home does not appreciate at all, the lender will have a 20% "cushion" against loss. If there is appreciation, the cushion will be even greater.

The lender needs that cushion to guard against loan losses. The smaller the cushion, the greater is the likelihood that there will be losses.

Remember, in an *uninsured* reverse mortgage, there are no insurance premiums to make up for loan losses. When there is no risk sharing, each individual loan must have a very low probability of loss. After all, one large loss could easily wipe out the gains on all other loans.

So uninsured lenders have to be *very* careful. And that means very definite limits on the loan term, and on the loan-to-value ratio.

Running the Numbers

Table 11 shows the monthly advance you could get from one of these loans if you chose a five-year term or a ten-year term.

The numbers assume a fixed interest rate of 10% and an 80% loan-to-value limit. In other words, at the end of the loan your debt will equal 80% of your home's value at closing.

The table also assumes you pay start-up costs in cash, and take no lump sum advance at closing. Creditlines and equity reserve accounts are generally not available with uninsured private loans.

As you can see, the amount of the monthly advance depends mostly on the length of the loan term that you select at closing. The shorter the term, the greater the loan advance will be.

This happens because you are spreading the same amount of equity over fewer months. So there can

Table 11: Uninsured Private Loan; Monthly Advances

Home Value at Closing	Maximum Loan Balance*	Monthly Advance for 5 Years	Monthly Advance for 10 Years
$50,000	$40,000	$512	$194
75,000	60,000	768	290
100,000	80,000	1,025	387
125,000	100,000	1,281	484
150,000	120,000	1,537	581
175,000	140,000	1,793	678
200,000	160,000	2,049	775
300,000	240,000	3,074	1,162

*In a typical uninsured loan, your debt (loan balance) at the end of the loan (in these examples, after five or ten years) cannot be more than 80% of the home's value at closing. The monthly advances are calculated so that the loan balance reaches this "loan-to-value" limit when the repayment date is reached. For example, $512 per month for five years at 10% interest will generate a debt of $40,000, which is 80% of the home's value at closing.

be more money in each advance. Also, the shorter the loan, the less time interest will have to compound. This means less of your loan balance will be interest - so more can be principal advances.

Table 11 does *not* show the impact of start-up costs and interest rates on loan advances. Turn the page, and we'll take a look at both.

What Do You Pay?

With an uninsured reverse mortgage, you don't have to pay any insurance premiums. This can reduce start-up costs to a point where you might consider paying them in cash. Because these loans have a fixed loan-to-value limit, you are very unlikely to end up "finessing" these costs.

Paying start-up costs with a lump sum advance at closing reduces the amount of your monthly advance. **Table 12** shows how much. Most uninsured loans have a fixed interest rate. Table 12 assumes the rate is 10%, and the loan-to-value limit is 80%.

Start-up costs other than insurance are generally similar to those on insured loans. Table 12 assumes these costs are about 2% of the maximum debt on your loan. It also assumes your home is worth $100,000 and the loan-to-value limit is 80%. So your maximum debt is $80,000, and 2% of that is $1,600.

Table 12: Uninsured Private Loan; Impact of Start-Up Costs on Monthly Advances

	Monthly Advance for 5 Years	Monthly Advance for 10 Years
Paying Cash for Start-up	$1,025	$387
Financing Start-up Costs	$957	$366

As you can see, the impact of financing your start-up fees is much greater when the loan term is shorter. That's because they are a larger part of your overall loan balance in the earlier years of the loan.

Over time, the cost gets spread out over many more monthly advances. So the impact on each is less.

Less Interesting Interest

The effect of interest rates on loan advances is shown in **Table 13**. This table is based on the same assumptions used in Table 11.

Perhaps the most surprising thing here is how little the interest rate affects the monthly advance. By contrast, small changes in forward mortgage rates make for large differences in your monthly payment.

Why should it be different for reverse mortgages?

Table 13: Uninsured Private Loan; Impact of Interest Rates on Monthly Advances

	Monthly Advance for 5 Years	Monthly Advance for 10 Years
Fixed Interest at 9%	$1,053	$410
Fixed interest at 10%	$1,025	$387
Fixed Interest at 11%	$997	$365

The main reason is that the scheduled term of these uninsured loans is much shorter than on a forward mortgage. With a shorter term, interest has less time to compound. So rate differences don't carry the weight they do on much longer loans.

TLC: Less, Then More

The Total Loan Cost method of looking at loan costs (see Chapter 14) works best when comparing risk-sharing loans to other risk-sharing loans. But the TLC concept can help you learn something about the general shape of uninsured loan costs, too.

On an uninsured private sector reverse mortgage, TLC rates start out lower than on risk-sharing loans with the same stated interest rate because

✓ the start-up costs are less on the uninsured loan; and

✓ the uninsured loan provides more money in loan advances due to its shorter term.

As a result, the total of all non-interest costs in the early years of the loan will be a smaller part of the uninsured loan's total loan balance. And that means a lower TLC rate.

But consider what could happen later on in the loan. Remember, the repayment requirement and the loan-to-value limit prevent your loan balance from ever reaching the value of your home at closing.

No Recourse to Non-Recourse

Say you live past your life expectancy and your home appreciates at a low rate, or not at all. In a risk-sharing loan, you would benefit from the non-recourse limit on the loan. This would drive your TLC rate *below* the stated rate on the loan.

But in an uninsured loan, you are very unlikely ever to benefit from the non-recourse limit in the same way. If your debt is never allowed to be greater than 80% of your home's value at closing, then it is very unlikely that your debt would ever reach the current value of your home.

What this means is that the TLC rate on your loan is very unlikely ever to fall below its stated interest rate. In fact, the TLC will probably always be greater than the stated rate.

By contrast, the TLC rate will fall *below* the stated rate on some risk-sharing reverse mortgages - the ones taken out by long-lived borrowers living in homes with moderate to low appreciation.

What's Left Over?

At the end of this loan you will owe some per cent of your home's value at closing. With a typical loan-to-value limit of 80%, your leftover equity would be 20% of your home's value at closing - minus any cost of selling your home, *PLUS* all the appreciation that occurs in your home's value during the loan term.

In other words, this loan has a kind of mandatory equity reserve built into it. Your debt can equal your home's value only if your home depreciates in value. Otherwise, you will end up with a nest egg of leftover equity when the repayment day comes.

But will it be enough? You can easily project what it *might* be using different appreciation assumptions. This could tell you, for example, what the best case and worst case might be.

But if you are thinking about an uninsured loan, you really need to make conservative assumptions and plan carefully.

By Whom? For Whom?

Given the serious risk problems for uninsured lenders and borrowers discussed earlier, which is the tougher question:

☐ What private lender would offer an uninsured reverse mortgage? or

☐ What consumer would take out such a loan?

Please, Sir, More Accrual

With few exceptions, lenders who make these loans are doing so in response to nonprofit and public agencies seeking to meet the needs of persons who are "house-rich, but cash-poor."

These advocacy efforts began in the early 1980s, and have led to a small number of uninsured reverse mortgage programs. Most of them started before private lenders figured out how to make the less risky insured loans.

Getting a Proper Fit

In most cases, the only way a lender would agree to make uninsured loans was if a nonprofit or public agency agreed

- ◆ to counsel all persons seeking them; and

- ◆ to screen out persons for whom an uninsured loan is inappropriate.

In particular, lenders and agencies agreed that the only people who should take out these loans are people who clearly expect and intend to sell or leave their homes prior to the repayment date. For example,

☐ an active homeowner on a waiting list to buy into a popular new congregate living facility;

☐ a recently widowed person whose income fell with her spouse's death, who intends to move at some point, but who needs some time before making any longer term decisions;

☐ a very frail and sick person who needs help to remain in her home for the year or two her doctors say she has left.

193

The advantages of the uninsured private loan in these types of situations are that

✓ they are less costly than risk-sharing loans in the short run;

✓ they can provide greater loan advances; and

✓ you get to keep all future appreciation.

Still, the risks of these loans are real and serious. Your best laid plans can change, or be messed up by unexpected events. At worst, an uninsured loan could end up forcing you out of your home.

Where To Get Them

Think one of these loans might fit your situation? If you do, you'll be disappointed by how few of these programs there are.

If your home is in one of the areas listed on the next page, check out the appropriate lender or agency for more detailed information.

If you home is not in one of these areas, you can try persuading a local lender to make one of these loans. But don't hold your breath.

A better approach would be to get pledges from friends and relatives to move their bank accounts to the lender you're trying to persuade - *if* the lender agrees to make you the loan. In that way you would be "funding" your own loan.

Table 14: Uninsured Private Loan Programs

STATE	AREA	CONTACT
Arizona	Northern Arizona	Reverse Mortgage Program 602-997-6105
	Southern Arizona	Reverse Mortgage Program 602-623-0344 (ext. 376)
California	Alameda and Contra Costa	ECHO Housing - RAM 415-930-0989
	San Francisco	Independent Living 415-863-0581
	San Mateo County	Human Investment 415-348-6660
	Santa Clara County	Project Match 408-287-7121
	Sonoma County	Sonoma Council on Aging 707-525-0143
	Southern California	Life Services 818-842-8555
Connecticut	Middlesex and New London	Farmers & Mechanics 203-346-9677
Massachu-setts	Massachu-setts	H.O.M.E. Program 617-924-6875
Minnesota	Mpls-St. Paul metro area	Senior Housing 612-645-0261
New Jersey	Bergen, Pas-saic, & Morris	Boiling Springs Savings 201-939-5000
New York	Nassau County	CHEC Program 516-485-5600
	Suffolk Co.	RAM Pgm; 516-427-1768
	Westchester County	Residential Housing Opps. 914-428-0953

Chapter 21

FHA Program Benefits

The United States Congress approved legislation to set up a federal reverse mortgage insurance program toward the end of 1987. It was signed into law by the President early in 1988.

The new law directed the U. S. Department of Housing and Urban Development (HUD) to develop and operate the program. The specific agency within HUD selected to run the program was the Federal Housing Administration (FHA).

How It Got Here

The FHA reverse mortgage insurance program is officially called the "Home Equity Conversion Mortgage Insurance Demonstration Program." It is the first free-standing insurance program for reverse mortgages ever developed.

The development process took all of 1988 and half of 1989. Final regulations were published on June 9, 1989 (Federal Register Volume 54, Number 110, pages 24822-24844). In the beginning, the program was limited to 50 lenders, and each lender was limited to 50 loans.

In the Spring of 1991, the program was expanded. Now, any FHA-approved lender can make FHA-insured reverse mortgages. There is no limit on the number of loans each lender may write. But there is an overall national limit of 25,000 reverse mortgages until September 30, 1995.

All Types of Advances

In Chapter 12 you learned about the different types of loan advances that reverse mortgages can provide: lump sums; lines-of-credit; monthly advances for a fixed term, or for as long as you live in your home.

Now would be a good time to take a quick look back at that chapter's description of these types of loan advances.

Did you look? It's on pages 88-91. The reason you might want to take a refresher peek is that the FHA program lets you

◆ choose any of these loan advance types,

◆ choose any combination of advance types, and

◆ change your loan advance plan in the future.

These choices make the FHA-insured reverse mortgage the most flexible and adaptable one currently available. This can be very helpful in tailoring a loan to individual needs.

Figuring the Amounts

The amount of the advances depends on the types of advances you choose. But it also depends on

✓ your age,

✓ the interest rate, and

✓ your home's value, which is subject to certain limits.

The program's lenders and counselors know how to figure out how much money you can get. They all use the same computer program. You just give them a few bits of information, and they will do the rest.

If you are not all that interested in *how* they figure out your advances, you could skip the rest of this section. The next section on "Analyzing the Amounts" will show you the basic pattern of how much money you can get. But if you want to see how the FHA program works, read on.

The "Principal Limit" Method

There are three basic steps in figuring out your loan advances:

1) use your age, home value, and interest rate to determine your "principal limit," which is the most cash you could possibly get at closing;

2) subtract from your principal limit any funds you need to use or set aside at closing, for example, to finance start-up costs or pay for repairs; and

3) use your "net" principal limit to figure out how much money you could get from any single type of loan advance, or any combina-tion of types.

Table Time

You begin by looking up your "principal limit fac-tor" in a table published by FHA (see **Appendix B**). You need two pieces of information to do this: your age, and the expected interest rate on the loan.

If you are married or if more than one person owns your home, you must use the age of the youngest borrower.

You get the "expected annual average interest rate" from your lender. If the lender is charging interest at a fixed rate (one that never changes), then that is the rate you use. If the lender is charging an adjustable (changeable) rate, then the "expected" rate is determined by an FHA formula* the lender must use.

The "Maximum Claim Amount"

After you find your principal limit factor, you have to find your "maximum claim amount." This figure is the lesser of

☐ the value of your home *OR*

☐ HUD's "203-b-2" limit for your area.

These 203-b-2 limits are dollar amounts set by HUD that are different in each area. In some rural areas, the limit is $67,500. In many urban areas, the limit is $124,875. In all other areas except Alaska and Hawaii, the limit is somewhere between these figures. In Alaska it is $135,000; in Hawaii, $180,500.

---

* The "expected annual average interest rate" equals the U. S. Treasury Securities rate adjusted to a constant maturity of ten years PLUS the "lender's margin." The lender's margin equals the initial rate on the loan MINUS the one-year Treasury rate. The purpose of this formula is to determine the financial market's best estimate of the average annual rate over the approximate term of FHA-insured loans. You can find the Treasury rates every Tuesday in the "Money & Investing" section of **The Wall Street Journal** in a small box called "Key Interest Rates."

The limit is called "203-b-2" because that's the part of the National Housing Act that defines it. From time to time, these limits are increased. FHA lenders know what the 203-b-2 limits in their areas are.

You need to be clear about what this limit means, however. It does *not* mean that you are ineligible if your home's value is greater than your 203-b-2 limit. It does mean that the amount of home value you can use to figure out your loan advances is limited.

In other words, if your home is worth $100,000 and your 203-b-2 limit is $80,000, then your loan advances will be the same as if your home were worth $80,000.

Go To The "Principal Limit"

Now that you know your principal limit factor and your maximum claim amount, you can figure out your principal limit. You do it by multiplication.

For example, if your age is 75 and your interest rate is 10%, then your principal limit factor is .416. If your home is worth $100,000 and your 203-b-2 limit is greater, then your maximum claim amount is $100,000.

To get your principal limit, you just multiply .416 times $100,000. The result ($41,600) is the largest possible lump sum of cash you could get from the loan at closing provided you pay all start-up costs out of your own pocket. In economics lingo, your principal limit is the "present value" of the loan advances available to you.

If you're like most people, however, you wouldn't take all the money you could get in a single lump sum at closing. But you probably would want to use some of your principal limit to finance your start-up costs, for example.

If we assume those costs are about 4% of your home's value ($4,000), then your "net" principal limit would be $37,600. That's the largest amount you could get in a single lump sum at closing if you finance your start-up costs.

Figuring Your Loan Advances

The net principal limit is also the number you use to generate all the other types of loan advances. You simply use the "time-value-of-money" formula built into most financial calculators.

For example, assume you want to put the full amount of your $37,600 net principal limit into a five-year term of monthly advances. You enter five years as the "N" or "term," $37,600 as the "present value," and 10.5% as the interest rate.

(You add 0.5% to the expected interest rate because the FHA insurance premium is charged in two parts: 2% at closing, plus 0.5% added to the periodic interest rate. Chapter 22 covers the cost of these loans in greater detail.)

You also set the calculator for "beginning of the term" because the monthly loan advances begin at closing. The answer in this example is $801 per month for a five-year term.

To calculate monthly advances for a tenure plan, FHA uses a "term" equal to 100 minus your age. For more details on calculating loan advances, see HUD Handbook 4235.1 (appendix 21) under **Resources.**

Analyzing the Amounts

Tables 15 and 16 show that the amount of money you can get from an FHA-insured reverse mortgage depends on your age at closing, and on the value of your home.

Table 15 displays the monthly loan advances you could get from a tenure plan, that is, for as long as you live in your home. **Table 16** shows the lines-of-credit you could get on a "standalone" basis, that is, with no monthly advances.

Table 15: FHA-Insured Loans; Impact of Age and Home Value on Monthly Advances for Tenure

	Tenure advance if home value equals . . .		
	$75,000	**$100,000**	**$125,000**
AGE			
70	$201	$274	$346
75	$259	$352	$444
80	$337	$455	$573
85	$446	$602	$757

Both tables assume that

✓ the interest rate is 10%,

✓ the 203-b-2 limit is $124,875,

✓ and you finance your start-up costs, which are 4% of your home's value.

Both tables show that the older you are at closing, the more money you can get from a reverse mortgage. They also show that the more your home is worth, the more money you can get.

But remember, *the 203-b-2 limits can have a very strong impact on your loan advances.* For example, on a home worth $250,000, you would get the same advances as you would on a home worth $125,000. Both exceed the table's 203-b-2 limit of $124,875.

Table 16: FHA-Insured Loans; Impact of Age and Home Value on Lines-of-Credit

	Creditline if home value equals . . .		
	$75,000	**$100,000**	**$125,000**
AGE			
70	$22,150	$30,200	$38,210
75	$27,700	$37,600	$47,451
80	$34,000	$46,000	$57,940
85	$40,675	$54,900	$69,054

Deploying Your Assets

The amount of money you can get also depends on the type of loan advances you choose.

Table 17 shows the monthly advances a 75-year-old borrower living in a $100,000 home could get. In particular, it shows the advances if she also takes a lump sum at closing or a line-of-credit. This table uses the same assumptions as Tables 15 and 16.

The two basic patterns in Table 17 are these:

◆ The longer the monthly advances are set up to run, the smaller the advances will be. Note that the smallest advance goes to the only "unknowable" term, that is, the tenure plan.

◆ The more money you take as a lump sum at closing or put into a creditline, the lower your monthly advance will be. Note that there is no monthly advance when you take the largest possible lump sum or creditline.

So how would you do it? What combination of lump sum, line-of-credit, and monthly advance would meet your needs? Would any of them? Or, would you put most or all of your available funds into just one of these types of advances?

As you can see, there are plenty of choices. And soon there will be one more.

Table 17: FHA-Insured Loans; Impact of Lump Sums and Creditlines on Monthly Loan Advances

	Monthly Advance If Term Is . . .			
	Tenure	15 Year	10 Year	5 Year
Any combination of a lump sum at closing and creditline totaling . . .				
0	$352	$412	$503	$801
$5,000	305	357	436	695
$10,000	258	302	369	588
$15,000	212	248	302	482
$20,000	165	193	235	375
$25,000	118	138	169	268
$30,000	71	83	102	162
$37,600	-0-	-0-	-0-	-0-

FHA is currently developing an equity reserve option. The final form of this feature may be a simple deduction from funds available at closing - like the lump sum and creditline. In other words, a fixed amount that becomes the last loan advance.

(If you skipped the "Figuring the Amounts" section, and are wondering where this "funds available at closing" came from, now would be a good time to turn back to page 199. It's not as forbidding as it might look. And you'll even learn some of the technical jargon used by your lender.)

Beneath the Surface

The FHA program has two unique features that make it worth more than its flexible loan advances. But they are not immediately visible to the naked eye.

Who Was That Bearded Man?

A decade ago, there wasn't much concern about bank failures. Now we know better.

You take out a reverse mortgage at a time in your life when you can't afford much if any risk. That's why you look so hard at the *lender* default clause and penalties in any private reverse mortgage contract.

If an FHA advance is paid late, the lender owes you a penalty equal to 10% of the advance. FHA lenders that default lose all interest earnings. And the FHA stands behind the lender, taking over the payment of loan advances to you if the lender fails.

Having Uncle Sam in your corner is the strongest guarantee against lender default that you are likely to find. And that's one feature that makes this loan worth more than meets the eye.

How Does Your Credit Grow?

The line-of-credit you establish at closing in the FHA program gets larger every month. It grows by the same rate as your loan balance is expected to grow.

Here is an example. Let's say you take out a credit-line of $10,000 at closing. If the expected interest rate is 10%, then your balance is scheduled to grow at 10.5% per year. (This includes the 0.5% "periodic insurance premium" you will learn about in the next chapter.)

If you do not use your line-of-credit at all during the first year of the loan, your available credit grows to be $11,102. If you do use some of the credit during the first year, then the amount you would have left would be $11,102 *MINUS* the amount of your advances plus the interest on those advances.

The basic point here is that an FHA creditline is not a fixed amount of money. It is a growing amount of money. And the rate it's growing at will most likely be more than enough to keep pace with inflation.

Over the length of your loan, your line-of-credit grows more and more. As the "interest" you "earn" compounds, your account gets larger at an ever-increasing rate.

So, once again, you get more than a first glance tells you.

Loan Costs & Expenses

As you have seen, the amount of your FHA loan advances depends on your age, your home value (up to the 203-b-2 limits), and the specific loan advances you choose.

Loan Costs

The amount of your loan advances also depends on the cost of the loan. **Table 18** shows how a monthly loan advance on a tenure basis can vary with different loan costs. It is based on a 75-year-old borrower living in a $100,000 home. It uses the same assumptions as Table 17.

As you would expect, the advances are larger when the costs are smaller. But the impact of these stated loan costs is probably not as great as you expected.

On the one hand, the start-up costs are expected to be spread out over a long period of time. On the other, the interest rates are not expected to compound for as long as they are scheduled to compound on forward mortgages.

Table 18: FHA-Insured Loans; Impact of Loan Costs on Monthly Advances for Tenure

	Tenure Advance When Interest Equals . . .		
	9%	**10%**	**11%**
Total Start-Up Costs As Percent of Home Value*			
3.5%	$379	$357	$334
4.0%	374	352	329
4.5%	370	347	324

* Or 203-b-2 limit, whichever is less.

Housing Expenses

An FHA-insured loan may include other expenses you need to be aware of and consider:

✔ property repairs, and

✔ property taxes and insurance.

These are a few of your favorite things, right? But now you get to decide how to enjoy them: paying in cash, or using your loan. If you use your loan, the amount of your advances will be less than if you pay for them with other funds.

Looks OK To Me

To be eligible for the FHA program, your home must meet HUD's "minimum property standards." This generally means that your home must not be in violation of any local building codes.

If your home does not meet HUD standards, then it must be repaired. If you use your loan to do it, the cost of the repair cannot be greater than the largest lump sum you could get at closing. If the cost equals your largest lump sum, of course, there wouldn't be any advances left in the loan after making the repair.

If the cost of the repair is less than 15% of your maximum claim amount (see page 201), then you can complete the repair work after the loan closes. But you will need a "repair rider" attached to your loan's legal papers to make sure that the work gets done.

Which Pocket?

An important decision you need to make before closing an FHA-insured loan is whether you want your property taxes and insurance paid from your loan.

It's your choice. You can either continue paying these expenses yourself, or you can ask the lender to pay them with your loan. If the lender uses your loan, then your monthly advances or your creditline will be reduced by that amount.

Be sure you decide how *you* want to handle this. If you do not tell the lender what you want, then the lender will subtract these expenses from your advances and pay them. If you do not want the lender to do that, you have to say so at closing.

Do not sign any loan documents unless you see your choice in writing.

And don't just focus on what you will get from the loan. Remember, you also need to understand what the loan will cost. What will the real, total interest rate be? How much equity will you have left over? Turn with me now to Chapter 22.

Chapter **22**

FHA Program Costs

FHA's reverse mortgage insurance program offers a wide range of benefits.

But you must understand that it is *not* a federal "giveaway" program paid for or "subsidized" by the taxpayers. It is a real insurance program paid for by the borrowers. In other words, the premiums you pay are computed to cover the real risk of loan losses.

The cost to you, therefore, can be substantial.

Checking the Checklist

In Chapter 13, you waltzed through the traditional checklist method of evaluating loan costs.

Now let's use that approach to learn the basic cost elements in an FHA-insured reverse mortgage. You may recall that the major cost categories were

☐ origination fees,

☐ third-party costs,

☐ insurance premiums, and

☐ interest charges.

Fees of Origin

The origination fee is set by each lender. But the program only permits the first 1% to be financed (paid for) with a lump sum at closing.

Most of the lenders in the early phase of the program charged a 1% origination fee. That means 1% of your home's value, or 1% of your area's 203-b-2 limit, whichever is less. In other words, 1% of the "maximum claim amount" (see **Glossary**).

This fee is where lenders cover their own costs and, they hope, make a profit. Most of the other charges they just pass on to others.

Party Supplies

Third-party costs are different in each area, but they can be fully financed with the loan. They include

✓ a property appraisal (generally a flat fee ranging from $150 to $250 which you may have to pay for before closing, but which may be paid back to you if your loan is approved);

✓ title search and title insurance;

✓ government fees for recording the mortgage;

✓ any legally required inspections (for example, for termites);

✓ servicing fee (can be charged as a flat monthly fee, or as part of the interest rate; more on this fee later in the chapter, on page 222).

A Two-Part Premium

The premium for FHA's reverse mortgage insurance coverage is charged in two parts:

♦ 2.0% of the maximum claim amount (home value or 203-b-2 limit, whichever is less) is charged at closing;

♦ 0.5% is added to the interest rate charged on the loan balance.

The "upfront" 2% charged at closing can be paid out of a lump sum advance. The "periodic" 0.5% is charged on your rising loan balance.

Verrrry Interesting

Lenders may charge either a fixed or an adjustable rate of interest on FHA-insured reverse mortgages.

♦ A fixed rate never changes. Your loan balance grows by the same rate every month.

♦ An adjustable rate does change (go up or go down). Each month your loan balance grows by whatever the current rate on your loan is.

Most lenders charge adjustable rates. If they do, they *must* offer an annually adjustable rate and they *may* offer a monthly adjustable rate.

☐ The annually adjustable rate cannot change by more than two percentage points each year. In addition, it cannot change by more than five percentage points over the life of the loan.

☐ The monthly adjustable rate cannot become greater than a maximum rate chosen by the lender and disclosed in your loan documents.

How It's Done

Changes in an adjustable rate have to follow FHA rules. Once the mortgage is closed, the lender cannot control changes in the interest rate. These changes are

216

determined by changes in an "index" that the lender must follow. The index is the U. S. Treasury one-year bond rate*. Here is how it's done.

The lender sets the initial interest rate when the loan is closed. The difference between this rate and the Treasury rate at that time is then established as the lender's "margin" on the loan.

Once it is set, the margin never changes. But when the time comes to change the interest rate (annually or monthly), the margin is simply added to whatever the Treasury rate is at that time to determine the new interest rate.

What It Does

Know what interest rate changes do to a *forward* mortgage? When the rate goes up, your monthly payment to the lender goes up. Sometimes by a lot.

That's why we generally prefer fixed rates, even if the adjustable rates start out lower. We don't like surprises. Especially the kind we can't afford.

But - as you have learned - reverse mortgages don't always behave exactly like forward ones. So you have to look at it with fresh eyes.

In an FHA-insured reverse mortgage, changes in the interest rate do *not* cause changes in your loan advances. What does change is the rate at which your loan balance grows.

---

* You can find the one-year Treasury rate every Tuesday in the "Money & Investing" section of **The Wall Street Journal** in a small box called "Key Interest Rates."

Finessing the Rates?

Adjustable rates are generally lower than fixed rates, and monthly adjustables are lower than annually adjustables.

The lower your interest rate at closing, the greater your loan advances will be throughout the loan. All other things being equal, therefore, the greatest advances go to the borrowers with the monthly adjustable rates.

When it is adjusted monthly, the actual interest rate will be lower at all times except when the limits on the annually adjustable rate loan would otherwise have been in effect. In other words, your rate would be lower during all the times that Treasury rate changes are less than two points per year and five points over the life of the loan.

And think about what happens if you live long enough - and your home appreciates little enough - that your balance reaches your non-recourse limit. If you did not take a monthly adjustable rate, you could end up owing the same amount but having gotten less in loan advances.

Different Risks

All in all, it's not the same set of interest rate risks you face on a forward mortgage. The reasons we prefer a fixed rate on a forward mortgage do not apply to a reverse mortgage. In any case, a creditline or equity reserve account is a more certain way to protect equity than choosing a less adjustable interest rate.

218

Similar to Forward Charges

Most of the stated costs on an FHA reverse mortgage are similar to those on most forward mortgages.

☐ The origination fee is probably lower on the FHA loan than on most forward mortgages.

☐ Most of the third-party costs are exactly the same as in forward mortgages.

☐ The insurance premium is roughly similar to FHA's forward mortgage insurance premium.

☐ The interest rate on these loans is probably similar to - or lower than - the rate on most forward mortgages.

All of the start-up costs together have ranged from about 3.5% to 5%, with an average of just over 4%. That's 4% of your home's value or your area's 203-b-2 limit, whichever is less.

If you home is now worth $100,000, for example, that would be about $4,000. If it's been a long time since you purchased your home, that's no doubt a lot more than you paid to set up your forward mortgage many years ago.

But today's stated cost of getting an FHA reverse mortgage on your home is probably roughly the same or less than today's cost of taking out a first-time loan to buy it.

With Some Differences

Although the overall stated cost of an FHA reverse mortgage is similar to that of most forward mortgages, there are some differences.

These differences are not present in all FHA-insured reverse mortgages, however. They come into play in the following areas:

✔ repairing your home,

✔ insuring your home,

✔ recording your mortgage, and

✔ servicing your mortgage.

Repairing

In Chapter 21, you learned that the FHA has certain minimum property standards. If your home does not meet them, then you have the added "cost" of making the repair.

Strictly speaking, this isn't a *loan* cost. But you have to make the repair to get the loan. If it's a repair you otherwise would not have made, then it probably seems more like a loan cost.

One way of reducing this cost, however, is to find a nice, low- or no-interest deferred payment loan. Then you might even come out ahead.

Insuring

A second type of "cost" appears if your home's fire and hazard insurance does not cover the current replacement value of your home. If it does not, you must update your insurance. The cost to do this, however, can be financed with the loan.

Again, if this is something you would not otherwise have done, it will seem like a loan cost to you. But it's a good idea for *you* to be fully protected, too. You've got your leftover equity to be concerned about.

Recording

A third potential cost may appear in the form of your state or local government's mortgage recording fee.

The method for calculating this fee is usually based on the forward mortgage. Sometimes that method can generate very high recording costs when applied to reverse mortgages.

That was not the intent of the people who wrote these laws in the first place. They were generally written long before anyone had even begun to think about reverse mortgages.

Often the agency collecting the fee can be persuaded to use the principal limit (see **Glossary**) to calculate the fee. Sometimes it requires a change in regulations or statutes to do this.

Servicing

In lender talk, "servicing" means everything they have to do after they set up or originate the loan. This includes

✓ making all types of loan advances to you

✓ transferring your insurance premiums to FHA

✓ keeping track of your loan balances (including any payments you make)

✓ sending you your regular account statements

✓ paying your property taxes and insurance at your request

✓ checking to make sure you are complying with all loan requirements (including occupancy)

✓ making any changes you request in your loan advance plan.

Often originating lenders do not service their loans. Instead, they transfer all or part of the servicing to a company that specializes in servicing. If they do so, they must give you the name, address, and phone number of a contact person with the servicer.

The cost of servicing the loan is not covered by the origination fee. It is either covered by the interest rate charged on the loan balance, or charged as a flat fee on a monthly basis. The typical monthly fee has been about $20 to $25. It can be automatically paid by your loan.

A Departure

On forward mortgages, the cost of servicing is almost always included in the interest rate. But then the size of the loan balance is very large and stable throughout most of the actual life of the loan. That means a small amount of additional interest can generate enough money to cover the cost.

On a reverse mortgage, by contrast, the balance is usually very small in the beginning and grows at a compounding rate. It would take a much greater amount of interest to generate the same amount of money for the lender. And it wouldn't be stable.

That is why FHA lets lenders charge a flat monthly servicing fee if they choose. In this way, they get a steady stream of income to cover their overall servicing costs. To keep things simple, the fee is generally the same on all loans.

But Clunky

But that means, for example, that you could pay a monthly servicing fee for the life of your loan even if 1) you took all of your available funds as a lump sum at closing, and 2) you paid all your property taxes and insurance in cash.

As reverse mortgage lending becomes more developed, other options for charging these servicing fees need to be found.

What Do You Pay?

As you know, there is a difference between the stated costs and the real costs on a risk-sharing reverse mortgage.

Reviewing the TLC

Here's a quick review of the particulars:

- ◆ The checklist method of cost analysis shows you which individual cost elements are *charged* to your loan balance.

- ◆ But it doesn't tell you how much you will end up *actually paying* for your loan in total.

- ◆ If you live in your home a short time, your total start-up costs (origination, most third-party costs, and the "upfront" insurance premium) will be a substantial portion of your overall loan balance.

- ◆ But if you live long enough - or your home appreciates little enough - your loan balance will reach your non-recourse limit (the value of your home).

- ◆ When that happens, the amount you owe depends on your home's value, *not* on the costs charged to your loan.

In short, the real, total cost depends on

✓ how long you live in your home, and

✓ what happens to its value.

The Total Loan Cost (TLC) is the annual average rate that includes *all* loan costs *AND* takes into account the non-recourse limit.

You can easily end up paying a much higher or a much lower Total Loan Cost rate than the interest rate charged on your loan balance. In the short run, risk-sharing loans are very expensive. But in the long run they can be a very good value.

Disclosing The TLC

When Congress authorized the FHA expansion in 1990, it required that lenders disclose the Total Loan Cost (TLC) rates on your reverse mortgage.

This means that the lender must show you in writing what these rates will be before you close your loan.

Remember, these are "projected" rates. In other words, they show what the rate would be *if* you live this many years (the loan term) and *if* your home's value grows by that much (the appreciation rate).

The form used to disclose the rates includes three loan terms and three appreciation rates. The terms show what the TLC rate would be

✓ after two years,

✓ at your approximate life expectancy, and

✓ at about 40% *past* your life expectancy.

The appreciation rates in the FHA disclosure show what the TLC would be if your home's value grows at 0%, 4%, and 8%.

Analyzing the TLC

Table 19 uses the same appreciation rates. But it provides a more detailed look at TLC rates over time. The figures are the same as in Table 6 in Chapter 14. You might want to turn back to that section (page 105) to review its detailed discussion of these rates.

Table 19: FHA-Insured Loan*; Total Loan Cost Rates

	When home value grows at . . .		
	0%	4%	8%
TLC rate after			
2 years	48.4%	48.4%	48.4%
7 years	14.8%	14.8%	14.8%
12 years	10.3%	12.3%	12.3%
17 years	3.7%	10.3%	11.5%
22 years	0.7%	6.1%	11.2%

*This mortgage provides $352 per month for as long as a 75-year-old borrower lives in her home, which is worth $100,000 at closing. Start-up costs are 4% of the maximum claim amount, and the expected average annual interest rate is 10%. This rate includes the servicing fee.

In general, Table 19 shows the real cost to be

✓ most expensive in the short run;

✓ less costly over time; and

✓ least costly if you outlive your life expectancy and your home appreciates at a moderate to low rate.

What's Left Over?

A simpler way of looking at loan costs is to see how much equity would be left at the end of the loan.

Leftover equity is also a key factor in planning for the future. If you are forced to move for health reasons - or if your situation changes unexpectedly in some other way - your leftover equity may become your single most important financial resource.

Table 20 shows how much would be left over after paying off the specific loan example used in Table 19.

In the FHA program, the full value of your home is available to repay the loan. But the lender may only realize the net sales proceeds. If your debt is $100,000 and your home sells for $100,000, the lender would get $100,000 if you sold the home yourself and had no selling costs. But if you paid a realtor 6%, for example, the lender would only get $94,000. The figures in Table 20 are the *gross* amounts available to the lender.

Table 20 shows the importance of appreciation. If there is none, you would run out of equity during the eleventh year of the loan. That is *less* than the life expectancy of the 75-year-old borrower in this case.

At a more moderate rate of appreciation (4%), you would not run out of equity until the 15th year. That's a bit longer than the *average* life expectancy of a 75-year-old borrower. But many people aged 75 at closing are expected to live at least that long.

Of course, if your home value grows at a more substantial rate (8%), you will have leftover equity throughout your loan. But hoping for high appreciation is not the surest way of preserving equity.

Table 20: FHA-Insured Loan*; Leftover Equity

End Year	Appreciation = 0%	Appreciation = 4%	Appreciation = 8%
2	$85,635	$93,795	$102,275
7	$47,914	$79,507	$119,296
12	0	$44,397	$136,111
17	0	0	$146,996
22	0	0	$139,673

*The mortgage in this table provides $352 per month for as long as a 75-year-old borrower lives in her home, which is worth $100,000 at closing. The start-up costs total 4% of the maximum claim amount (in this case, 4% of $100,000), and the expected average annual interest rate is 10%. This rate includes the servicing fee. "End year" means end of year.

Taking the Sure Way

There is a way to be certain that you will have some equity if you have to move in the future.

You take out a line-of-credit, and any of it you do not use will be left over for future use. If you have to sell and move, you can withdraw the full amount of your remaining credit before paying off the loan.

Because the creditline grows over time, you can end up with more credit than you started out with. For example, if the borrower in Table 20 takes a $10,000 line-of-credit at closing, it would reduce her monthly advance to $258.

But if she does not use the creditline, it would grow to be nearly $48,000 after 15 years - the year her equity would run out if her home appreciates at 4%. In other words, taking about $100 less per month in this case would give the borrower $48,000 more left-over equity after 15 years.

Even a $5,000 creditline would grow to nearly $24,000 after 15 years. The "cost" in this case would be about $50 less per monthly loan advance.

Chapter **23**

FHA Program Availability

Who can get these FHA-insured reverse mortgages? And where can you get them?

The answer to the first question is very clear and definite. This chapter lays out the basic rules on qualifying for these loans.

But the answer to the second question is still developing. The program started small and is now beginning to expand. This chapter shows you how to find participating lenders, and light a fire under others.

Are You Eligible?

To qualify for an FHA-insured reverse mortgage, both you and your home must eligible.

All owners of your home must be aged 62 or over. At the time of closing, at least one owner must be living in the home as a principal residence. If you owe any debt against your property, it must be less than your FHA principal limit.

There are no limits on your income, assets, or other resources in the FHA program.

Counseling Required

Before you can close an FHA reverse mortgage, you must receive counseling from a HUD-approved counseling agency. Your lender will give you the names, addresses, and phone numbers of approved agencies in your area.

The counseling is required by the federal law that set up the program. By statute, it must cover the following topics:

✓ the financial consequences of reverse mortgage borrowing;

✓ reverse mortgages other than the FHA program, for example, deferred payment loans, property tax deferrals, uninsured and lender-insured private loans;

✓ options other than reverse mortgages, for example, health and social service programs, income support programs, and various housing options; and

✓ a disclosure that reverse mortgages may affect your estate, your taxes, and your eligibility for state and federal government programs.

The purpose of the counseling is to help you be an informed consumer. That means helping you think through your situation, and understand the choices that are available to you. Once you've read this book, however, you'll probably be a better candidate to be a counselor than a counselee.

In any case, FHA counselors have been advised *not* to make decisions for you, and *not* to lead you to any particular conclusions. Their job is to help you clarify and understand your options.

Is Your Home Eligible?

Your home must be an existing one-unit property. Mobile homes, duplexes, triplexes, and cooperative units are not eligible.

Condominiums and planned unit developments (PUDs) are eligible, however, *if* they are part of a HUD-approved project. Each HUD field office has a list of HUD-approved projects. You can find the nearest HUD field office by calling 202-708-1112.

If your condo or PUD is not HUD-approved, the field office can tell you how to get HUD approval. The requirements for condos are in HUD Handbook 4265.1. The requirements for PUDs are in HUD Handbook 4135.1 (REV 2, Appendix 9).

Your home also must meet HUD minimum property standards. This usually means your home may not violate any government building codes. If it does, you must correct the violations to get the loan.

The repairs can be financed with your loan, provided they do not cost more than your principal limit. If the repairs cost less than 15% of your maximum claim amount, you can complete them after closing.

Where Are The Lenders?

There are about 10,000 FHA-approved lenders in the United States. In May of 1991, *all* of them became eligible to make FHA-insured reverse mortgages.

But there is a difference between "eligible to make" and "making." In order to make reverse mortgages, lenders need to know

- ◆ what reverse mortgages are,

- ◆ what reverse mortgage insurance is, and

- ◆ that they are eligible for FHA reverse mortgage insurance.

234

At this point, however, you already know much more about reverse mortgages than most lenders do. You know that federal reverse mortgage insurance protects lenders against the risk of loan losses. And you also know that the FHA insurance is available to all FHA-approved lenders.

Unfortunately, most FHA-approved lenders still do not even know what a reverse mortgage is. Most of the lenders who do know, however, could not tell you what reverse mortgage *insurance* is. The number that know they are *eligible* for FHA reverse mortgage insurance is very small.

So - there's work to be done. But before getting into the details of educating lenders, let's take a look at the pioneering lenders in the FHA fold.

Leaders of the Pack

When the first phase of the FHA program started, only a handful of lenders volunteered to participate. And of the ones selected by the federal government, only about half stayed with the program.

In the early going, it wasn't easy, and it certainly wasn't profitable. Any new program has start-up problems that need to be worked out. This one required quite a bit of learning: new concepts, new procedures, new working relationships, new consumer needs to be met. Fortunately, there were enough lenders with the vision and perseverance to get it off the ground.

235

You may live in an area served by one of these pioneering lenders listed in **Table 21**. They lend only in the state or states for which they are listed. And they do not always lend all over those states.

Table 21: FHA-Insured Reverse Mortgage Lenders

STATE	FHA LENDER
Arizona	Directors Mortgage; 714-652-4326
California	ARCS Mortgage; 800-237-2727
	Bank of Lodi; 209-367-2075
	Directors Mortgage; 714-652-4326
Colorado	Wendover Funding; 303-843-0480
Connecticut	Prudential Mortgagee; 516-565-3000
Delaware	International Mortgage; 301-484-6016
DC	International Mortgage; 301-484-6016
Florida	Sterling Savings; 407-968-1000
Georgia	Capital One Mortgage; 404-934-9790
Hawaii	ARCS Mortgage; 800-237-2727
Indiana	Merchants Mortgage; 317-237-5158
Iowa	Commercial Federal; 402-390-5155
Kansas	James B Nutter; 816-531-2345
Maine	ME State Housing; 207-626-4600
Maryland	International Mortgage; 301-484-6016
Minnesota	Executron Mortgage; 612-854-7676
Missouri	James B Nutter; 816-531-2345

Nebraska	Commercial Federal; 402-390-5155
Nevada	Directors Mortgage; 714-652-4326
N Hampshire	Chittenden Bank; 802-660-2123
New Jersey	Interchange State Bank; 201-845-5600
New Mexico	Charter Bank; 505-291-3758
	Sunwest Bank; 505-765-2211
New York	ARCS Mortgage; 800-237-2727
	Onondaga Savings; 315-424-4011
	Rockwell Equities; 516-334-7900
	Prudential Mortgagee; 516-565-3000
Oregon	ARCS Mortgage; 800-237-2727
Ohio	Mid-America Mortgage; 216-861-4040
Pennsylvania	Boulevard Mortgage; 215-331-6900
	International Mortgage; 301-484-6016
	Landmark Savings; 412-553-7727
	Mid-America Mortgage; 216-861-4040
	Pioneer Mortgage; 609-546-1700
Rhode Island	RI Housing & Mortgage; 401-751-5566
S Carolina	First Citizens Mortgage; 803-733-2747
Vermont	Chittenden Bank; 802-660-2123
Virginia	International Mortgage; 301-484-6016
	VA Housing; 804-782-1986
Washington	ARCS Mortgage; 206-292-8853
W Virginia	International Mortgage; 301-484-6016
	Mid-America Mortgage; 216-861-4040
Wyoming	Key Bank; 307-635-7724

Driving Misdoubt

Reverse mortgage lending has always been a "consumer-driven" idea. Lenders have been slow to understand and believe that retirement income could be "home-made."

If there are no FHA reverse mortgages available in your area now, there probably will be in the future. How far in the future will most likely depend on

✓ how many consumers ask lenders in your area if they offer reverse mortgages,

✓ how many consumers actively encourage these lenders to offer reverse mortgages, and

✓ how much these lenders learn about reverse mortgages from these consumers.

So - how do you go about educating your lenders and driving out their doubts about reverse mortgage lending? There are two basic movements:

1) you need to understand your lender's point of view; and

2) you need to know the specific steps that can lead your lender from "being eligible to make" reverse mortgages to "making" them.*

---

* In Texas, lenders are unlikely to join the FHA program until a legal issue regarding constitutionally-prohibited mortgage debt is resolved.

The Lender's Perspective

Private sector lenders have never been opposed to the *idea* of reverse mortgages.

They understand that the population is aging. They know that home equity is the single largest asset held by retired Americans. They would like to do more business in this area.

Many believe reverse mortgages may be part of the natural next stage in the development of the financial services industry. They have built up a long-term relationship with their customers, and they would like to extend it into the retirement years.

Barriers to Business

So what's been holding them back?

Practical things. Serious, down-to-earth, everyday-business barriers to this new kind of lending. Basic problems that wouldn't go away, and had to be solved before more lenders could be realistically expected to do "reverse" lending.

The good news, however, is that these practical problems have now been identified - *and solved.*

But that has only happened quite recently. Most lenders don't know that it's happened. They have no idea how simple and safe it's become to make reverse mortgages that meet consumer needs.

Let's review what the problems were, and how they've been solved. In short, the three most serious barriers to reverse mortgage lending have been:

☐ the lack of reverse mortgage insurance,

☐ the lack of a secondary market, and

☐ the lack of contract servicing.

Understanding the Barriers

As you have learned, reverse mortgage insurance manages the risk of loan losses. Prior to the FHA program, this type of insurance was not available to lenders. That meant they could only offer uninsured loans, or develop their own insurance. For most lenders, neither of these was a practical choice.

On forward mortgages, most lenders get the money they lend from the "secondary" mortgage market, a network of institutions in the business of buying and selling mortgages. Until recently, however, there was no secondary market for reverse mortgages. As a result, lenders had to put their own funds at risk.

Computerized systems are necessary for the efficient servicing of mortgage loans. But the cost of developing new systems doesn't make economic sense for individual lenders. And until recently, no company specializing in loan servicing had offered such servicing on a contract basis. This meant that reverse mortgage servicing would be a very costly item for most lenders.

Prior to the FHA program, reverse mortgage lending was a very difficult if not practically impossible business for most lenders to get into. It required much more than just adding a new "product" to their array of financial services.

In truth, it required most of the activities normally involved in *creating* a new and complex product *PLUS* starting a new business.

Bashing the Barriers

All that began to change in 1989, however. That's when three key developments occurred that smashed the major barriers to reverse mortgage lending:

◆ a federally-guaranteed reverse mortgage insurance program was unveiled by FHA;

◆ a secondary market program to fund reverse mortgages was announced by the Federal National Mortgage Association ("Fannie Mae"); and

◆ a contract servicing plan for reverse mortgages was initiated by Wendover Funding of Greensboro, North Carolina.

These breakthroughs have completely changed the climate for reverse mortgage lending. Now these loans are just as safe, just as liquid, and just as serviceable as any forward mortgage. The federal government insures the risk, the secondary market supplies the funds, and a subcontractor services the loans.

Remaining Concerns Small

Compared to the major barriers that have been removed, the remaining concerns for lenders are quite manageable.

✔ They need to learn the ins and outs of the FHA insurance program (FHA handbooks are available, and training seminars are offered by Barrentine Lott & Associates; 703-764-3070).

✔ They may want to arrange for secondary funding and contract servicing (with Fannie Mae and Wendover Funding, respectively).

✔ They need to ready their legal documents (FHA prototypes are available).

✔ They need to develop local marketing strategies and adapt promotional materials.

Seven Steps to Lending

But how do you get them started?

Try this seven-step plan. You can try the first six steps on your own. The seventh step may or may not be necessary or helpful.

Or, you could *begin* with step seven, and involve others in your efforts from the start. That may be a less direct approach, but it might be more effective.

1) Find an FHA Lender

First you need to find any bank, savings association, mortgage company, or credit union that makes FHA loans of any kind. All FHA-approved lenders are eligible to make FHA-insured reverse mortgages.

Your best bet is probably a locally-owned lender. Then your concerns are less apt to be referred to a higher level in a different city. Other good prospects:

✓ lenders with whom you are currently doing business or have done business in the past;

✓ lenders that have some sort of "club" or other program for retired customers;

✓ lenders with especially strong reputations as "good citizens" in your community;

✓ lenders with a solid reputation for service.

You can often tell if lenders offer FHA loans by looking at their ads in the yellow pages. Or you can just call them up and ask.

2) Find the Right Person

Ask to speak to the person in charge of mortgage lending. If it's a small lender, it may be better to ask for the president or the manager. If the lender is large enough to have a mortgage department or mortgage subsidiary, ask to speak to the person who runs it.

243

3) Say What You Want

Tell the lender you are interested in getting an FHA-insured reverse mortgage. Ask if they have seen "HUD Mortgagee Letter No. 91-1 (page 5)" that makes *all* FHA-approved lenders eligible to make FHA-insured reverse mortgages.

4) Cover the Basics

Tell the lender these loans

◆ are fully insured by the federal government;

◆ can be funded by Fannie Mae; and

◆ can be serviced by Wendover Funding of Greensboro, North Carolina.

5) Ask for Action

Ask the *lender* to do three things:

✓ contact the nearest HUD field office (call 202-708-1112 for location and number); ask for HUD Handbook 4235.1, Mortgagee Letters 90-17 and 91-1, and 24 CFR 206;

✓ call the nearest Fannie Mae regional office for a copy of its "Home Equity Conversion Mortgage Information and Instruction Package";

✓ call Wendover Funding at 919-668-7000 for information on its reverse mortgage start-up services.

6) Check Back

Call back in a week or two to see if the lender got the materials from HUD, Fannie, and Wendover.

After the materials arrive, ask for the lender's reaction to them. Ask what steps have to be taken for the lender to offer reverse mortgages. Volunteer to discuss the matter with any other decision-makers involved.

7) Show Support

Get community organizations and agencies to support the development of a reverse mortgage lending program in your area.

They could invite lenders to a meeting to discuss the proposal. They could follow up with the lenders who show the most interest. They could write letters attesting to the community credit needs that reverse mortgages can meet.

Other Strategies

But what do you do if you have no FHA lenders in your area, or if all the FHA lenders in your area refuse even to consider making reverse mortgages?

☐ Contact your state housing finance agency (HFA), and encourage it to become a reverse mortgage lender. HFAs in Maine, Rhode Island, and Virginia are making FHA-insured loans possible in their states.

☐ Encourage a non-FHA lender interested in reverse mortgages to become an FHA-approved lender. The process isn't difficult. Your nearest HUD office has details.

☐ If your community has substantial numbers of persons in need of reverse mortgages, you could document this fact and present your findings to local lenders. Each year they must file a report telling how they are meeting the credit needs of their communities in compliance with the Community Reinvestment Act (CRA). Your research could help them find new ways of fulfilling their CRA obligations - through reverse mortgage lending.

Chapter 24

Lender-Insured Programs

The FHA-insured reverse mortgage was not the first one to manage the risk of loan losses through a premium charge.

There have been other private sector, risk-sharing reverse mortgages. In these plans, the *lender* develops the risk-sharing mechanism, collects the premium charges, and covers any loan losses. In lender-insured reverse mortgages, there is no separate insurer such as the FHA. The lender manages the risk directly.

Lift-Off in New Jersey

The very first type of risk-sharing reverse mortgage featured "shared appreciation." Although not currently being offered, this plan was available through most of the 1980s in about a dozen states. Modified versions of it are likely to reappear in the future.

How It Worked

The "Individual Reverse Mortgage Account" was developed by a New Jersey company called American Homestead. The IRMA plan charged a fixed rate of interest and a premium related to growth in the home's value over the life of the loan. It also let you mortgage less than the full value of your home, thereby reserving some constant percent of your home's value.

If the home did not appreciate, *OR* if the loan balance reached the non-recourse limit, then no premium was owed. On the other hand, if the home did appreciate *AND* the loan balance fell short of the non-recourse limit, then the premium would equal the *lesser* of

☐ the difference between the loan balance and the non-recourse limit, or

☐ the appreciation on the percentage of home value that you mortgaged.

This formula produced a very wide range of TLC rates. In the short term - or with high appreciation -

the rates were very high. But in the long term, with low to moderate appreciation, the rates were very low.

These loans had substantial monthly advances. The 75-year-old borrower in a $100,000 home who gets about $350 per month on a tenure basis from an FHA loan got $500 per month from American Homestead. A later entrant - the Providential Home Income Plan of San Francisco - provided $530 per month.

Why It Paused

Neither of these companies is a depository institution. Neither has deposits made by savers that they can lend out to borrowers. Both companies are brokers between their borrowers and larger lending institutions. So they must get very large, long-term loans to have the funds to make a lot of reverse mortgages.

During the 1980s they could get these loans. Larger lenders were willing to fund "shared appreciation" mortgages because they expected that homes would appreciate at a moderate to substantial level.

But in 1990, when overall appreciation expectations dropped (and a recession began), funding for new shared appreciation mortgages dried up. Future versions of these plans are likely to be less dependent on appreciation or provide lesser loan advances.

Meanwhile, if appreciation is low in the 1990s, some of the people who took out these reverse mortgages during the 1980s may end up having gotten the best deal of all.

The Capital Holding Plan

The first major financial services corporation to make reverse mortgages was Capital Holding Corporation of Louisville, Kentucky.

With more than $11 billion in assets and $43 billion of life insurance in force, Capital Holding is among the 10 largest investor-owned life insurance companies in America.

Availability

In the Fall of 1988, Capital Holding began offering its reverse mortgage plan in parts of Virginia, Maryland, and Kentucky.

Today the plan is available throughout those states, California, and Florida. Late in 1991, it is expected to become available in the greater Chicago area - Cook, Lake, Kane, and DuPage counties.

To be eligible for this plan, you must be aged 62 or older, and your home must be worth at least $75,000. Single family homes and condominiums are eligible. But any current debt against your home must be paid off with a lump sum at closing.

What Do You Get?

Capital Holding provides monthly advances for as long as you live in your home. The loan must be repaid when you die, sell, or permanently move.

Despite advertising "income for life," this plan does not continue providing monthly advances if you move out of your home.

You may also get a lump sum at closing or a line-of-credit account in addition to the monthly advances. But the larger the lump or the line, the smaller the monthly advance will be. You may not get just a lump sum or just a creditline without the monthly advances.

The Capital Holding plan permits you to mortgage less than the full value of your home. In this way you can preserve equity for the future. But don't get this feature confused with Capital's creditline, which it calls a "reserve account."

Loan Advance Amounts

Table 22 shows the amount of monthly advances for single borrowers who finance all their closing costs, who mortgage the full value of their homes, and who take neither a lump sum nor a creditline.

In general, these amounts are greater than the FHA's monthly advances on a tenure basis. But they are less than the advances formerly available through the shared appreciation type of reverse mortgage.

You can use the numbers in Table 22 to figure out the approximate loan advances on homes of greater value.

For example, to find the monthly advance for a 75-year-old borrower living in a $150,000 home, simply double the amount for a 75-year-old living in a $75,000 home.

Table 22: Capital Holding Plan; Monthly Advances for Single Borrowers

	Tenure advance if home value equals . . .		
	$75,000	**$100,000**	**$125,000**
AGE			
70	$255	$340	$425
75	337	450	562
80	438	585	731
85	560	747	933

* Advances for homes of other values are approximately proportional to the figures in this table. For example, a 75-year-old could get about $787 on a home worth $175,000. "AGE" means "age at closing."

Couples Get Less

Table 23 shows an important difference between the Capital Holding plan and the FHA program. In the FHA program, the advances are based on the age of the youngest borrower. This means that a 75-year-old single borrower would get the same advances as a couple aged 75 and 80.

In the Capital plan, the couple would get a lower monthly advance. Table 23 shows how much less.

It assumes that joint borrowers (for example, married couples) are the same age. In other words, a 75-year-old couple includes a husband and wife each aged 75. If the ages are different, then the further apart they are, the closer their advances would be to the ones for the younger age in Table 22.

Table 23: Capital Holding Plan; Monthly Advances for Joint Borrowers

	Tenure advance if home value equals . . .		
	$75,000	**$100,000**	**$125,000**
Age			
70	$192	$257	$321
75	259	346	432
80	342	456	570
85	442	590	737

* Advances for homes of other values are approximately proportional to the figures in this table. For example, an 80-year-old could get about $798 on a home worth $175,000.

The reason for treating joint borrowers differently is that their life expectancies are longer. The result is that the monthly advances for joint borrowers in the Capital Holding plan are very close to the ones offered by the FHA program.

A detailed comparison of the FHA and Capital Holding plans is presented in Chapter 27.

Deploying Your Assets

If you take a lump sum at closing or set up a line-of-credit, your monthly advances will be less than those in Tables 22 and 23.

Table 24 shows the impact of lumps and lines on the monthly advances of a single 75-year-old borrower living in a $100,000 home. If there is no lump or line, the monthly advance on a tenure basis is $450.

But the monthly advance is reduced by about $50 for every $5,000 put into a lump sum at closing or a creditline. And the amount of either a lump or line is limited in this case to a maximum of $18,000.

Unlike the FHA line-of-credit, the Capital Holding creditline does *not* get larger over time. It is a fixed amount that decreases as you use it.

All other things being equal, this makes Capital's lump sum at closing a better deal than its creditline. Each has the same impact on your monthly advance. But a reinvested lump sum would earn interest.

Table 24: Capital Holding Plan; Impact of Lump Sums and Creditlines on Monthly Advances *

	Monthly Advance for Tenure
Lump sum at closing or creditline in the amount of . . .	
0	$450
$5,000	399
$10,000	348
$15,000	297
$18,000 (maximum)	263

* Assumes a 75-year-old single borrower living in a $100,000 home.

Preserving Some Equity

The Capital Holding plan lets you preserve some of your equity for future use by you or your heirs after your loan is over.

It does so by letting you decide at closing *how much* of your home to mortgage. They call this the "applied" home value, that is, the percentage of value you want applied to the mortgage. In other words, you can set aside a percentage of value that is *not* applied to the mortgage, and which remains with you.

For example, a 75-year-old living in a $100,000 home could get $450 per month on a tenure basis. However, if she decides to mortgage only 80% of her home's value, then her monthly advance would be about 20% less ($360). But she would preserve 20% of her home's future value. A more detailed example of this important feature is discussed in Chapter 27.

What Do You Pay?

The Capital Holding plan requires a $100 application fee which is refundable if your loan closes. You also must pay for any recording fee or mortgage tax.

All other start-up costs are included in a flat $3,000 closing and origination fee, plus a 7% "guarantee" charge. The 7% is charged on your "applied" home value, that is, the amount of equity being mortgaged.

If you die before the total of the loan advances you have received reaches the total of the $3,000 plus the 7%, the difference is refunded to your estate.

A Period of Adjustment?

The annually adjustable interest rate charged on the loan balance is 2.5% over the 10-year U.S. Treasury securities rate. Changes in the interest rate do not affect your monthly advances or available creditline. But they do affect the rate at which your debt grows and, therefore, the amount of leftover equity.

An optional 6-point cap on the interest rate over the life of the loan is available. But it reduces the monthly payment by a significant amount. The 75-year-old borrower living in a $100,000 home who gets $450 per month with an uncapped rate would get $410 per month with a capped rate.

It would only save her equity if and during the times the rate exceeds the 6-point cap. Meanwhile, she would be getting $40 less every month throughout the life of the loan. If rates do exceed the cap, then it is more likely that loan balances will reach home values.

And, as we have seen, if that happens you will be better off having selected the greater advances that come with more adjustable rates. Surer ways of preserving equity are to establish a creditline or mortgage less than the full value of your home in the first place.

Non-Recourse, Of Course?

When it comes to cost limits, a non-recourse is a non-recourse of course of course, unless it belongs to Capital Holding. Then it's more complicated - but well worth your effort to understand. So don't recuse yourself from this non-recourse discourse.

Here's how it works.

The amount you owe at the end of the loan is the *least* of the following three amounts:

☐ your loan balance at that time;

☐ 93% of the "applied" home value at that time, that is, the applied home value at closing plus all the appreciation on that value, times 93%; or

☐ the "projected" home value, which is the applied value at closing increased by the change in the Consumer Price Index (CPI) plus 1.3% annually over the course of the loan.

That's a mouthful of techni-talk. But it can mean big savings. So listen up.

Unraveling the Recourses

Paying 93% of an applied value is less than paying 100% of full value. For example, if you only mortgage 80% of your home's value, then you can never owe more than 74.4% of its full value (80% X 93%).

But you could owe even less. The "projected" home value limits the amount you owe to the debt you would have if your home appreciated at the national average appreciation rate. In other words, if your home appreciates at a rate higher than the national average, you get to keep the "above average" appreciation. This means your loan costs less, and you retain more equity.

The formula used by Capital Holding is based on the historic relationship between the "all-items" CPI-Urban index and home prices. In the past, home prices have exceeded this index by about 1.3%. If your home performs better than that, your TLC rates will be lower and your leftover equity will be greater.

Running the Numbers

Tables 25 and 26 show the TLC rates and leftover equity on a Capital Holding reverse mortgage.

As in the FHA plan, the TLC rates in **Table 25** are greatest in the early years when start-up fees are a larger part of the total amount owed. By the end of year 12 - the approximate average life expectancy of the borrower - the rates range from 5.7% (at zero appreciation) to 13.7% (at 8% appreciation), with a "most likely" figure of 12.4% (at 4% appreciation).

Table 25: Capital Holding Plan*; Total Loan Cost Rates

	When home value grows at . . .		
	0%	**4%**	**8%**
TLC rate after			
2 years	72.5%	72.5%	72.5%
7 years	18.3%	18.3%	18.3%
12 years	5.7%	12.4%	13.7%
17 years	0.2%	7.3%	10.0%
22 years	-2.3%	5.1%	7.7%

* Assuming a 75-year-old mortgaging the full value of her $100,000 home; assuming no lump sums and no creditlines; assuming the CPI-Urban index averages 4%.

Remember, TLC rates include *all* loan costs plus the security of monthly advances and no repayment until death, sale, or permanent move-out.

Table 26 presents the leftover equity on the same loan example used in Table 25. You are always left with at least 7% of the applied home value because you can never owe more than 93% of that amount. In this example, that means you always retain a minimum of $7,000. If you sell your home yourself and have no selling expenses, then you get to keep the $7,000.

Table 26 also shows the dramatic impact of Capital Holding's "projected" home value limit. If your home appreciates at 8% per year, and the CPI-Urban index rises at 4%, you retain a substantial amount of equity - especially if you outlive your life expectancy.

Table 26: Capital Holding Plan*; Leftover Equity

	When home value grows at . . .		
	0%	**4%**	**8%**
End of Year			
2	$75,610	$83,770	$92,250
7	23,244	54,837	94,626
12	7,000	11,207	86,740
17	7,000	13,635	129,409
22	7,000	16,589	232,178

* Assuming a 75-year-old mortgaging the full value of her $100,000 home; assuming no lump sums and no creditlines; assuming the CPI-Urban index averages 4%.

Lender Default

If Capital Holding fails to make a loan advance, the borrower must notify the company in writing. The company then has 90 days in which to come up with the money. If it doesn't, it is in default. The contractual penalty for lender default is limited to

✓ forgiveness of all interest due from the date of closing through the date of default; and

✓ forgiveness of the upfront fees ($3,000 plus 7% of the applied home value).

The borrower still has no obligation to repay the loan until death, sale, or permanent move-out. The legal enforceability of these lender default provisions has not yet been tested.

Future Developments

Capital Holding has the only lender-insured private reverse mortgage loan at present. But they won't for long. Other products are currently being developed. Still others are being retooled for reintroduction.

When Part FIVE takes you shopping for reverse mortgages, Chapter 29 will take a look at the future of these plans.

Part

FIVE

Shopping for Reverse Mortgages

Chapter **25**

To Thine Own Self

The two basic rules when considering a reverse mortgage are

◆ know thyself, and

◆ take your time.

Put another way, "to thine own self be true," even if it takes a while to figure out exactly what that means. It's your equity, and it's your needs that count.

Your Needs Come First

Any major decision you make should fit *your* situation and meet *your* needs. It should be based on a full understanding of all the choices available to you, and their consequences.

The biggest risk is that you might make a decision *before* you figure out your true needs, or *before* you understand what your real options are.

For starters, then, you must be very clear about what your financial needs are.

- ☐ Do you really need more money every month for regular expenses?

- ☐ Do you really need a large lump sum of cash?

- ☐ Are you doing fine each month, but need more cash now and then for irregular expenses?

- ☐ Do you have a specific need such as a home repair or improvement?

- ☐ Are property taxes a major burden?

- ☐ Are you concerned about future health costs?

- ☐ Do you want to leave some equity for heirs?

- ☐ What *amounts* of cash do you need?

An Overall Plan

Financial needs are only one part of the picture. You also must consider all your other needs - housing, health, social - and the full array of options available for meeting them. What is the overall cost of each solution? And what are the consequences of each?

All things considered, which solutions make the most sense to you? With which solutions are you most comfortable?

Many excellent books on financial planning and retirement planning can help you think through some of the larger issues involved. **Part FIVE** of this book looks at how reverse mortgages might fit into your overall plan. It considers the following questions:

◆ What options other than reverse mortgages might be better choices (**Chapter 26**)?

◆ How do you compare reverse mortgages (**Chapter 27**)?

◆ What are some of the other financial effects of reverse mortgages (**Chapter 28**)?

◆ What new forms of reverse mortgages are likely to develop in the future (**Chapter 29**)?

◆ What types of situations have led people to consider reverse mortgages (**Chapter 30**)?

Shopping for Reverse Mortgages

When you first start thinking about taking out a reverse mortgage, it isn't at all clear that you need one. The idea may sound interesting, but the best solution to your financial situation may be something else entirely.

That's why you need to consider the other options discussed in **Chapter 26,** and the various publications listed in the **Resources** section.

If you've read everything up to this point, you know more than most people about reverse mortgages. **Chapter 27** provides a quick review and summary comparison of these loan plans.

Some of the financial consequences of reverse mortgage borrowing are considered in **Chapter 28.** They include the impact of these loans on heirs, taxes, and public benefit programs.

Smart shoppers are always on the look-out for new and improved products. **Chapter 29** takes a peek into the near future of reverse mortgage lending.

It's usually helpful to hear about others who are considering similar decisions. So **Chapter 30** presents short looks at typical situations that have led people to consider reverse mortgages.

And finally, the **Appendixes, Glossary,** and **Resources** sections provide additional information and materials for you to consider.

Chapter 26

Other Options

Don't skip this chapter.

You might find something you hadn't considered.

But if you don't find anything new, you'll at least have considered a variety of options other than reverse mortgages.

And that will give you a better sense of what your real alternatives are.

The other options considered in this chapter involve housing, services, income, and debt. In each area, *excellent booklets and other materials are available for investigating specific options in greater depth.*

These other publications are listed in the **Resources** *section (see page 333).*

Housing Options

You are probably interested in reverse mortgages because you want to remain living in your own home just as you have always done.

But have you fully considered the possibility of selling and moving, selling and staying, or adapting or sharing your home?

Selling and Moving

What could you sell your home for? How much would you have left after paying any selling costs and any taxes you might owe? (Remember, if you are 55 or over, you may be able to exclude up to $125,000 of any gain on the sale of your home from federal taxes.)

Where would you move? What would it cost you to move? Would you buy or rent? What would it cost you to live? How would your new home compare to where you are living now?

Even if you are certain you do not want to move, it's a good idea to figure out the answers to these questions anyhow. It will tell you what your financial situation would be if you did move.

You can then compare that to your financial situation at present, and to what your situation would be if you took out a reverse mortgage or chose one of the other options discussed in this chapter.

You can only compare the costs of different choices by figuring out what they would be. And you just might be surprised.

Take A Look

Maybe you could get more for your home than you thought. Maybe there is another housing arrangement that would meet your needs as well or better. You really owe it to yourself to do some exploring.

In brief, your choices might include

✓ buying a less costly home;

✓ renting an apartment;

✓ buying or renting a unit in a congregate living facility or retirement community; or

✓ moving into a shared housing or group home situation.

Buying a new home means being responsible for its upkeep and maintenance. But you probably would be better able to afford hiring help with the money you make from selling your current home.

The basic difference between the first two choices and the others is that the others may have some built-in services. For example, meals, housekeeping, chore services, transportation, recreation and social events.

These services can make life more comfortable. But maybe you could get them in your current home.

You really need to consider how supportive your home, neighborhood, and community are now. Is it easy to manage your home? Can you get the goods and services you need? Do you have the family and social contacts you want?

If your answers are "yes", would you have to give any of this up if you moved? If your answers are "no", could you do better elsewhere? At what cost?

Selling and Staying

Although it is not easy, it is possible to sell your home and remain living in it.

There are two ways of doing this. The first one is called a "sale leaseback." In this type of deal, you sell your home and then rent it from the buyer on a long-term lease.

The buyer gives you a downpayment and pays off the rest of the purchase price over time. So you earn interest. And, since the payment you get from the buyer each month is greater than the rent you pay, you come out ahead. In addition, you are no longer responsible for taxes, insurance, and maintenance.

Sounds good, but it's hard to find a buyer who will accept these conditions. Since 1986, federal tax law has been less favorable to sale leasebacks than it had been prior to that time. There just isn't as much federal tax subsidy in the deal as there used to be.

Today, sale leasebacks work best within extended families. The National Center for Home Equity Conversion publishes a "Sale Leaseback Guide and Model Documents" (see the **Resources** section).

Life Estates

The other type of sale plan is a "life estate." That's what lawyers call "ownership until death." What you actually sell is "ownership upon death" - or what attorneys call the "remainder interest."

In other words, you remain the owner for the rest of your life. Upon your death, the person who bought the "remainder interest" becomes the owner.

This deal has even fewer federal tax advantages than the sale leaseback. At present, attempts are being made to develop a workable for-profit program. But so far, none has been successful.

A form of life estate is offered by some nonprofit organizations: hospitals, universities, churches. But it usually involves the *donation* of a remainder interest. It only works if your income is great enough to get a substantial tax deduction for your charitable donation.

But even then you have to be very careful. What you get out of these deals may be far less than you could get from some reverse mortgages.

271

Analyzing Sale Plans

The best way to compare a sale leaseback or life estate plan to a reverse mortgage is to pretend it *is* a reverse mortgage.

Look at the money you would net after income taxes and - in the case of a sale leaseback - the expenses you would no longer have: property taxes, insurance, maintenance. Pretend all these amounts are loan advances.

Then use these "advances" to project TLC rates based on what you would "owe" if the transaction were to end at various points in the future. Also look at your leftover equity position at those points.

Make certain the contract has strong penalties against default by the buyer. If the plan includes an annuity, be sure to consider the issues raised about annuities in Chapter 29.

Adapting or Sharing

Have you considered renting out part of your home?

It can bring you new income, companionship if you want it, and another set of hands to help with keeping up your home.

You can create a self-contained "accessory apartment" within your home, or simply rent out a room. Some local agencies have matching services that help you find compatible renters.

272

Services Options

Services that help you stay in your home are available in most communities. The types of services and their costs vary from one area to another. Often they are available on a low-cost or no-cost basis.

The best place to find out about these services is usually your nearest area agency on aging (AAA), city or county office on aging, or senior citizen center. If you can't find any of these agencies, call your state unit on aging, and ask for help in locating them.

Table 27: State Units on Aging; Telephone Numbers

AL	205-242-5743	GA	404-894-5333
AK	907-365-3250	HI	808-548-2593
AZ	602-542-4446	ID	208-334-3833
	800-352-3792	IL	217-785-2870
AR	501-682-2441		800-252-8966
CA	916-322-5290	IN	317-232-7020
CO	303-866-5905		800-545-7763
CT	203-566-3238	IA	515-281-5187
	800-443-9946		800-532-3213
DE	302-421-6791	KS	913-296-4986
	800-223-9074		800-432-3535
DC	202-724-5622	KY	502-564-6930
FL	904-488-8922	LA	504-925-1700
	800-342-0825	ME	207-626-5335

Table 27: State Units on Aging, continued

MD	301-225-1102	ND	701-224-2577
	800-338-0153		800-472-2622
MA	617-727-7750	OH	614-466-5500
	800-882-2003	OK	405-521-2327
MI	517-373-8230	OR	503-378-4728
MN	612-296-2770	PA	717-783-1550
	800-652-9747	RI	401-277-2858
MS	601-949-2070		800-752-8088
	800-222-7622	SC	803-735-0210
MO	314-751-3082		800-922-1107
	800-235-5503	SD	605-773-3656
MT	406-444-3111	TN	615-741-2056
	800-332-2272	TX	512-444-2727
NE	402-471-2306		800-252-9240
NV	702-486-3545	UT	801-538-3910
NH	603-271-4390	VT	802-241-2400
	800-852-3311		800-642-5119
NJ	609-292-4833	VA	804-225-2271
	800-792-8820		800-552-4464
NM	505-827-7640	WA	206-586-3768
	800-432-2080		800-422-3263
NY	518-474-4425	WV	304-348-3317
	800-342-9871		800-642-3671
NC	919-733-3983	WI	608-266-2536
	800-662-7030	WY	307-777-7986

You need to find out which services are available, and how much they would cost. Maybe you can afford to buy them without having to take out a reverse mortgage. On the other hand, a reverse mortgage may give you the funds to do so.

Although they vary from place to place, services that support independent living generally fall into one of three categories:

☐ at-home support services,

☐ at-home health services, and

☐ community support services.

At-Home Support Services

Do you think the Beatles were talking about at-home support services when they sang "I get by with a little help from my friends"?

Probably not. But those words are as good a definition of these services as you'll find. Here is a quick list of the types of help they can provide:

◆ cleaning,

◆ laundry,

◆ shopping,

◆ meal preparation,

◆ yardwork,

◆ household chores,

◆ home maintenance work,

◆ meals-on-wheels,

◆ home visits and phone calls,

◆ emergency alert programs, and

◆ at-home care for a relative to give the main caregiver a break (usually called "respite" care).

At-Home Health Services

Needing the services of a healthcare professional doesn't mean you have to go to a clinic, hospital, or nursing home anymore.

Those of us who remember "house calls" are especially pleased to see the growth of home health care agencies. These agencies don't send doctors to your home. But then we don't always need doctors for what ails us.

If what you need can be provided by a nurse, therapist, or personal attendant, then you should look into the services of the home health care agencies in your area. Look under "home health services" or "home health care" in the yellow pages. Or ask your doctor.

Home health care agencies usually provide several types of *therapy* in your home:

◆ physical therapy,

◆ respiratory therapy,

◆ occupational therapy, and

◆ speech therapy.

They also generally provide *personal care services* such as

◆ bathing,

◆ dressing,

◆ feeding, and

◆ mobility; and

nursing services such as

◆ injections,

◆ dressings, and

◆ supervision of medicines.

Many agencies also provide nutrition counseling and durable medical equipment.

Case Management

Some home health care agencies take on the overall responsibility for finding and coordinating the variety of services that might be needed in a given case. This is called "case management" or "care management."

Many state governments also provide case management services. Often there is a program to help people figure out a plan of at-home and community services to help them keep out of a nursing home. Contact you area agency on aging or state unit on aging for details.

Or contact the National Association of Private Geriatric Care Managers at 602-881-8008.

Community Support Services

A variety of outside-the-home services can make it easier for people to remain living independently at home. These include

◆ adult day care and other respite care services,

◆ congregate meal programs,

◆ specialized transportation systems that accommodate wheelchairs and walkers, and

◆ support groups for dealing with various conditions and situations.

Contact you area agency on aging or state unit on aging for details.

Income Options

Most people who are eligible for Social Security and Medicare have already signed up for them at their nearest Social Security office.

But that's not the case with several other programs that provide cash income or help with expenses.

SSI Alert

Ever get one of those sweepstakes mailings that says "You may already have won!"? Well, if your income is low and your assets are limited, you may already be eligible for a program you may never have heard of.

In fact, roughly half of all the people eligible for this federal program have not signed up for it. Most of them have never heard of it or they don't know they are eligible for it.

The program is *Supplemental Security Income*, and is usually called *SSI*. It provides a cash payment every month to low-income persons who are aged 65 or over, blind, or disabled. To be eligible, your income and assets must be below certain levels, which are different in each state.

Contact your Social Security office for details about SSI in your state. You can get regular Social Security *and* SSI if you qualify for both. That's why it's called "supplemental" security income.

SSI is especially important because your eligibility for other programs may depend on your being eligible for SSI. In other words, signing up for SSI may make it easier for you to sign up for other programs.

Other Income Options

Your area agency on aging and state unit on aging can fill you in on other income programs available in your area.

Be sure to ask about medicaid, tax relief, and energy assistance.

☐ *Medicaid* covers the cost of certain health care expenses for persons with low incomes and limited assets. In most cases, this program is available through a county health or social services agency.

☐ *Tax Relief* of various types is available from federal, state, and local governments. Contact the Internal Revenue Service (IRS), your state revenue or taxation department, and your local property tax collector for details. Be sure to ask your local government about property tax rebates, exemptions, and credits.

☐ *Energy Assistance* programs provide help with heating, cooling, and weatherizing expenses. Contact your area agency on agency or community action agency for details.

Debt Options

To qualify for traditional types of debt - second mortgages, home equity loans, refinanced first mortgages - you must have enough income to make the monthly repayments that are required.

If you have that kind of income, and if you can *easily* afford to make the required monthly repayments, then you should at least consider these types of loans. If you intend to sell and move in a few years, then you should definitely give it some thought.

Proceed With Caution

Compare the amount of money you could get from these loans versus a reverse mortgage. If you need a large lump sum, a reverse mortgage may not generate as much cash as you need.

Look at the cost of setting up the loans, and compare the interest charges. Will changes in an adjustable rate affect the amount of your monthly repayments?

Check to see if you must "requalify" for the loan each year. If your spouse dies and your income is reduced, for example, could you be forced to repay the loan in full? What are your rights if you miss a loan repayment? What are the lender's rights?

For a closer look, get a free copy of "Borrowing Against Your Home: The Risks, Pitfalls and Advantages of Home Equity Loans" (D12987) from AARP Fulfillment, Box 3401, Lakewood CA 90801.

Chapter 27

Reverse Mortgage Options

Now that we've reviewed options other than reverse mortgages, let's summarize and compare the various reverse mortgage plans.

Table 28 shows the five basic types of reverse mortgage discussed in **Part FOUR**. In particular, it summarizes information about the availability, costs, and benefits of these plans.

Take a minute to refresh your memory.

Table 28: Reverse Mortgage Features

	Deferred Payment Loan	Property Tax Deferral
Offered by	local government housing agencies or nonprofit organizations	local tax collectors in CA, CO, CT, FL, GA, IL, IA, MA, ME, NH, OR, TX, UT, VA, WA, WI
Income requirement?	yes	yes
Loan advance types	one-time lump sum	annual lump sum
Limits on use of loan advances?	home repairs and improvements only	property tax payment only
Repayment requirement	at death, sale, or permanent move	at death, sale, or permanent move
Start-up costs	low or none	low or none
Interest	0% to 6% simple; fixed rate	6% to 8% fixed; usually simple
Lender default protection	not applicable	not applicable

Table 28, continued

Uninsured Reverse Mortgage	FHA-Insured Reverse Mortgage	Lender-Insured Reverse Mortgage
private lenders in AZ, CA, CT, MA, MN (metro), NJ (Bergen), NY (Nassau, Suffolk, Westchester)	private lenders in 32 states at present (6/91); about 10,000 lenders are eligible for the program	Capital Holding in CA, FL, KY, MD, VA, and (in Fall of 1991) IL; other plans currently being developed
no	no	no
monthly for a fixed term; optional lump sum	monthly tenure or term; standalone or optional credit-line or lump sum	monthly tenure or term; optional creditline or lump sum
no	no	no
when loan advances stop	at death, sale, or permanent move	at death, sale, or permanent move
closing costs, origination fee	closing costs, origination fee, insurance	closing costs, origination fee, insurance
market rate; fixed	market rate; fixed or adjustable	market rate; adjustable
generally none	guarantied by the U.S. government	default penalty in loan contract

Basic Program Features

The basic features of these plans will be major factors in determining which, if any, you might select. For example, if the only financial problem you want to solve right now is financing a home repair or paying your property taxes, then a public sector loan may be an obvious choice.

Or if you need more income for a short time before you sell and move, then an uninsured reverse mortgage might make the most sense - if you can find one.

If you have no need for additional monthly income, but you do need a substantial lump sum or creditline, then the FHA program may be a logical selection.

But what if you are looking for a monthly income supplement that continues for as long as you live in your home. How would you choose between the FHA program and one or more lender-insured plans?

Side By Side

A good place to start is to put the answers to our three little questions side by side, and compare

◆ What can you get from each program?

◆ What would each cost?

◆ What would you have left over?

What Do You Get?

Table 29 compares the monthly loan advances you could get on a tenure basis from the FHA and Capital Holding plans.

The FHA advances are the same for single borrowers and joint borrowers. This makes the FHA plan more competitive for joints than it is for singles. Single persons can get much larger advances every month from the Capital Holding plan.

203-b-2 or not 203-b-2

Table 29 also shows you the impact of FHA's 203-b-2 limits.

To get Capital Holding advances for homes worth more than $125,000 you *add* the figures for lower-valued homes. For example, a single person aged 75 living in a $150,000 home gets about double what a single person living in a $75,000 home gets.

But with the FHA plan, all homes that exceed the 203-b-2 limits in their areas generate the same advances as the 203-b-2 limits do. So, for example, the 75-year-old single person in Table 29 could never get more than $444 per month - no matter how much her home is worth.

Single persons living in homes valued at more than the 203-b-2 limits in their areas can get substantially greater monthly advances from the Capital Holding plan. The more the home exceeds the FHA limits, the greater the difference between the monthly advances.

*Table 29: Comparison of Monthly Tenure Advances**

	Tenure advance if home value equals . . .		
	$75,000	**$100,000**	**$125,000**
	FHA - CH (*joint*)	FHA - CH (*joint*)	FHA - CH (*joint*)
Age			
70	201 - 255(*192*)	274 - 340(*257*)	346 - 425(*321*)
75	259 - 337(*259*)	352 - 450(*346*)	444 - 562(*432*)
80	337 - 438(*342*)	455 - 585(*456*)	573 - 731(*570*)
85	446 - 560(*442*)	602 - 747(*590*)	757 - 933(*737*)

*CH = Capital Holding. All figures taken from tables 15, 22, and 23 on pages 204, 252, and 253, respectively.

Growth versus No-Growth

But this doesn't mean that the Capital Holding plan will always provide more funds. Remember, the FHA creditline grows, and the Capital line does not.

Consider this example, which is based on Table 17 (page 207) and Table 24 (page 254).

Borrower A and borrower B are each 75 years old, and each lives in a $100,000 home. Borrower A takes the FHA plan in two parts: a monthly tenure advance of $305 plus a $5,000 line-of-credit. Borrower B takes the Capital Holding plan in two parts: a monthly tenure advance of $297 and a creditline of $15,000.

Who gets the most funds? Depends on how long they live, and what they do with their creditlines.

Table 30 shows what would happen if each borrower lives to her actuarial life expectancy (about 12 years) and then cashes in her full line-of-credit.

The FHA borrower gets the most funds. In addition to getting $305 per month for 12 years, she gets a creditline cash-out of about $17,500. That's what happens when $5,000 grows at 10.5% for 12 years.

By contrast, the Capital borrower gets less each month ($297) and has less left in her creditline. That's what happens when $15,000 doesn't grow at all for 12 years.

You could take out the full amount of the Capital creditline at closing and place it in an interest-bearing account. But the after-tax interest it earns would most likely be at a rate lower than the one at which FHA's creditline grows. And the account would be counted as a liquid asset in most public benefit programs (see page 300).

Table 30: Comparison of Tenure Advance and Creditline*

	FHA	Capital Holding
Tenure advance	$305	$297
Creditline at closing	$5,000	$15,000
Creditline at life expectancy	$17,500	$15,000

* Based on Table 17 (page 207) and Table 24 (page 254). See text for other assumptions.

What Do You Pay?

Table 31 compares the TLC rates for the FHA and Capital Holding plans. It combines Table 19 (page 226) and Table 25 (page 258).

Table 31 assumes a 75-year-old borrower who mortgages the full value of her $100,000 home and takes the maximum monthly loan advance. It also assumes that both loan balances grow at 10.5%, that start-up costs on the FHA loan are 4%, and that the CPI-Urban index increases at 4% per year.

Comparing TLC Rate Patterns

In both plans, TLC rates are based on the largest potential debt. In the FHA plan, this reflects the fact that the full value of the home is available to repay the loan. In the Capital Holding plan, the debt is limited to 93% of the applied home value, or less.

Prior to life expectancy (about 12 years), the FHA plan has the lower TLC. After life expectancy, the Capital Holding plan has the lower overall cost.

At life expectancy, it depends on appreciation. If the rate is very low (0%), then the Capital Holding cost is lower. If the rate is high (8%), then the FHA cost is lower. And if the rate is moderate (4%), then the cost is about the same.

In short, you can put aside all the specific cost elements and non-recourse variations in these plans. Which costs less? Depends primarily on how long you live in your home.

Table 31: Comparison of TLC Rates*

	When home value grows at . . .		
	0%	**4%**	**8%**
	FHA - CH	**FHA - CH**	**FHA - CH**
TLC rate after			
2 years	48.4 - 72.5	48.4 - 72.5	48.4 - 72.5
7 years	14.8 - 18.3	14.8 - 18.3	14.8 - 18.3
12 years	10.3 - 5.7	12.3 - 12.4	12.3 - 13.7
17 years	3.7 - 0.2	10.3 - 7.3	11.5 - 10.0
22 years	0.7 - (2.3)	6.1 - 5.1	11.2 - 7.7

* See text on top of page 290 for assumptions.

What's Left Over?

Tables 20 and 26 (pages 228 and 259) displayed the amount of equity you would have left if you took out the *maximum* monthly loan advance on a tenure basis from each plan: $352 from FHA; $450 from Capital Holding.

Table 32 compares leftover equity if you take out the *same* monthly advance from each plan: $352. Taking this lower monthly advance from Capital Holding means you can preserve some of your equity, or put it into a creditline or a lump sum advance at closing.

In Table 32, we assume you choose to preserve all the equity that you don't put into monthly advances.

In other words, you mortgage less than the full amount of your home's value. As a result, Capital Holding's leftover equity figures are greater in Table 32 than they were in Table 26.

In fact, reducing the Capital advance to $352 lets you preserve $21,750 at closing. Then, even if your home's value never changes, you always retain this initial "non-applied" value *PLUS* 7% of the applied value (7% X $78,250 = $5,478) for a total of $27,228.

If your home does appreciate, your leftover equity will be greater than that. And the stronger the appreciation, the more equity you will have left.

Table 32: Comparison of Leftover Equity - Equal Tenure Advances ($352)*

	Leftover equity if appreciation equals . . .					
	0%		4%		8%	
	FHA	CH	FHA	CH	FHA	CH
End yr.						
2	85,635	80,114	93,795	88,274	102,275	96,754
7	47,914	38,597	79,507	70,191	119,296	109,980
12	0	27,228	44,397	43,592	136,111	120,392
17	0	27,228	0	53,037	146,996	181,738
22	0	27,228	0	64,526	139,673	299,925

* CH = Capital Holding. Same assumptions as Table 31 except in this CH loan the applied home value is $78,250.

This comparison is an example of the short-cut cost analysis method discussed in Chapter 15. If both plans provide the same cash benefit, then the one with the greater leftover equity costs less. Compare Table 32 with Table 31. You'll see that the overall pattern of leftover equity is the same as the TLC cost pattern discussed on page 290.

Reserve versus Lump or Line

When you decided to take $352 per month from Capital Holding, you didn't have to preserve the rest of your equity. You could have chosen a lump sum at closing or a line-of-credit instead.

If you did that, you could have gotten $352 per month plus a lump or line equaling $9,600. How would this compare with $21,750 in preserved equity? Depends on when you ask.

If you invested the full amount of a lump or line at closing in an account earning 8%, and if your home appreciated at 4%, then your $9,600 account would grow twice as fast as your $21,750 in equity reserve.

But it would take about 22 years for the invested funds to catch up to the more slowly-growing amount in the equity reserve. And that assumes you would never withdraw any of the invested funds.

So the trade-off is between return and liquidity. You would be most likely to end up with more funds at a future date in this example with an equity reserve than with an invested lump sum. But you would not have direct access to the funds until the loan is over.

Capital Holding does not permit refinancing a loan to access preserved equity. But it will permit you to borrow against that equity from another lender.

In addition, any appreciation in the value of an equity reserve is non-taxable and non-countable by public benefit programs.

Ying and Yang

Although the final form of FHA's equity reserve feature has not yet been made public, an interesting development may be brewing.

It is likely that FHA's equity reserve will permit you to preserve a fixed *amount* of equity. The Capital Holding plan, as we have seen, permits you to reserve a fixed *percentage* of equity.

In other words, your reserve account grows (when your home appreciates) in the Capital plan. But it is likely not to grow in the FHA program.

That's just the opposite of what the creditlines in each program do. FHA's line grows, but Capital's does not.

Perhaps some day we'll see a plan in which the consumer can decide whether to designate a fixed amount or a fixed percentage in both areas.

Other Issues

Comparing private sector reverse mortgages involves the kind of side-by-side financial analysis you've just looked at.

But you also need to consider factors such as the future flexibility and long-term security of each plan.

The FHA program lets you change your loan advances at any time for a fee that cannot be greater than $20. For example, you could switch from a monthly advance to a creditline, or vice versa. You could add a creditline to a monthly advance, or vice versa.

These types of changes could be very important if your situation changes. Financial flexibility is worth something. Only you can decide how much.

Security is also important. If your lender misses a loan advance, would you rather write a letter, wait up to 90 days, and possibly go to court - or would you rather be the recipient of a 10% late fee, and have Uncle Sam standing behind your lender?

Again, only you can decide how much these features are worth to you. Are greater flexibility and security worth the lower advances you might get in the FHA program? Or would you rather have the extra cash every month?

Probe, Push, Tune, Tweak

Negotiating is an important part of comparing.

Is the deal you're being offered really the best the lender can do? Are there parts of the financial details or legal documents that give you pause? Could you do better in some of these areas with other products?

Would the lender consider changing this figure or that clause?

You need to do some of this probing and pushing just to get a full and complete picture of the deal as initially offered. But you should also do it for three other reasons:

✓ you may end up getting a better deal;

✓ many other homeowners may end up getting better deals if the changes made for you are then built into the product; and

✓ you may be helping the lender develop a better product that will mean more satisfied customers and more customers that are more satisfied.

At this stage in the development of reverse mortgages, lenders have their ears to the ground. It's a new product and a new business. They don't know what will be most attractive to which consumers.

So they are listening carefully. What do consumers want? Which combination of features will generate the most sales? How can they improve their products to attract more customers?

So go ahead. Help them out. Tell them exactly what you like and what you don't like. Tell them what would have to be different for you to sign on the dotted line. Fine-tune the deal to your specific needs.

Chapter 28

Other Financial Effects

By now you are well aware that a reverse mortgage is serious business.

It takes what may be your most important financial asset and turns it into cash, loan costs, and - especially if you plan for it - leftover equity.

The main financial consequences of this transaction have been discussed in earlier chapters. Now let's consider the timing and destination of the equity you convert into cash.

Now or Later?

In one sense, reverse mortgages present you with familiar issues. When should you cash in a financial asset? How much should you use now, and how much should you save for later?

It's the same basic question you face with a savings account, pension, CD, IRA, stock, bond, or other investment. The more you use now, the less you will have left in the future.

If you could see the future, it would be a lot easier. But you don't know how long you will live and what your real needs will be. So you lean to the conservative side, and make the best decisions you can.

With A Twist

Reverse mortgages provide an interesting variation on this general theme.

Should you take out a reverse mortgage now? Or wait until later?

If you wait, you will be older when you take out the loan, and your home will probably be worth more. Unless loan costs rise sharply, this means you will be eligible for greater loan advances. If loan costs drop, the advances will be even larger.

On the other hand, if your home's value falls and loan costs rise, you may end up with smaller advances despite being older.

If you take out a private sector reverse mortgage, you can decide how much equity you want as cash now versus how much you want to "save" for the future. The various types of loan advances plus equity reserve accounts make this "now or later" decision a key part of reverse mortgage planning.

Yours or Heirs?

This may involve deciding whether you want to share any of your equity with others - and *when* you want them to get it.

Some people assume that reverse mortgages mean your heirs get nothing. In fact, most private plans have let you decide *how much* of your equity to use yourself, and how much to give or leave for others.

Some borrowers have used part of an initial lump sum to make an "early" bequest. Others have drawn on a creditline to help out heirs sooner rather than later. Still others have used equity reserve accounts to preserve equity for distribution by their estates.

Yours or *Theirs*?

How does the government treat reverse mortgages?

This book does not provide legal advice. And any current government policy is subject to change. Your own legal advisor is your best source of information.

But we can report what the American Bar Association has found in developing its "Attorney's Guide to Home Equity Conversion" (see **Resources**).

In general, loan advances that you receive are not taxable. On the other hand, however, the interest on a reverse mortgage is not deductible during the time it is being charged to the loan. Ordinarily, deductions are not available until interest is actually paid by you.

If you expect there will be a large capital gain on the eventual sale of your property, you should take special care to evaluate the potential consequences. If you expect the gain will exceed your one-time federal tax exclusion of $125,000, you may want to preserve enough equity to cover your tax liability.

Public Benefit Programs

If you are receiving government benefits that are based on your financial situation, you need to know that reverse mortgages may affect your benefits.

Your eligibility for Social Security and Medicare is *not* based on your income and assets. The benefits from these programs are *not* affected, therefore, by the receipt of reverse mortgage advances.

But if you are receiving SSI, for example, you need to understand how your loan advances are treated. In the federal SSI program, loans are not considered to be income. But, if you retain any advances past the end of the calendar month in which you receive them, they are counted as a "converted resource."

In other words, if you put your loan advances in a savings or checking account, and don't spend them before the end of the month in which you receive them, they will be treated as a "liquid asset." And if you want to retain your eligibility for SSI, your liquid assets may not exceed $2,000 for a single person, $3,000 for a couple.

A Helpful Rule

This rule is a good one. It means you should never get more money from a reverse mortgage than you actually need to spend.

Remember, if you borrow funds only to put them away in a savings account or other investment, you are no doubt losing money. The interest rate you pay on any private loan is going to be greater than the rate you could safely earn on your funds.

Public reverse mortgages, on the other hand, are limited to helping you with specific expenses - and investing is clearly not one of them.

A Common Rule

Federal SSI rules are often used by states on any supplement they provide to the federal SSI program and on their medicaid programs.

However, if you receive either of these benefits or any others that depend on your financial situation, don't assume the federal SSI rules are the ones being used. Check with each program to see how it treats loans.

Being aware of the rules can make all the difference. For example, a homeowner receiving SSI and medicaid could temporarily lose both benefits if she borrowed $4,000 for a new roof on September 25 and paid the roofer on October 5.

But she would *not* lose her benefits if she borrowed the $4,000 on October 1 and paid the roofer on October 10. Why? Because in this case she would not be retaining the loan advance past the end of the calendar month in which she received it.

So the key in this case is scheduling. But you can't plan ahead if you don't know the rules. So if you are getting benefits that depend on your financial situation, be sure to find out if a loan will affect your benefits.

Your area agency on aging and state unit on aging can help you get the information you need.

Chapter 29

Looking Ahead

Did you buy the last of the HI-FIs or the first of the stereos? Did you switch your savings from a passbook account to a money market fund? Do you prefer the tried and true, or are you always looking for the latest breakthrough?

No matter what their leanings, smart shoppers keep an eye on the future. When will which products become available in your area? Are much better versions about to come out? Will that reduce prices on current models? Should you buy now, or wait a bit?

Forging the Future

There are two ways of looking to the future: from
the stands, or from the field. This section reviews the
more activist approaches that have been suggested in
earlier chapters.

If what you need is a deferred payment loan, and
none is available to you, there is a reasonably good
chance you could get a program started (see Chapter
18). Many local agencies have found these programs
to be an important part of local housing policy.

A property tax deferral program, on the other hand,
is much more difficult to justify, design, and operate.
And it usually requires state legislative action. It is
also very difficult to get a private lender to develop
an uninsured reverse mortgage loan program.

Supporting Insured Plans

If no FHA lenders in your area are making reverse
mortgages, you should try out the action plan in Chapter 23. Consumers have led the way in all previous
stages in the development of reverse mortgages.
That's not likely to change anytime soon.

If you are a member of a pension fund, you can
support the development of lender-insured private
plans. Pension funds are the most logical source of the
long-term debt these plans need. You can encourage
both the benefits and investment professionals who run
your pension fund to explore this opportunity.

Recent Breakthroughs

In Chapter 23 you learned about all the recent breakthroughs that have occurred through the FHA program:

☐ federal insurance,

☐ funding by Fannie Mae,

☐ servicing by Wendover Funding, and

☐ eligibility for about 10,000 FHA lenders nationwide.

You also learned that these breakthroughs are only now starting to hit the awareness of lenders. In fact, it will take some time before the number of lenders actually making these loans grows significantly.

No Changes Expected Soon

What all this means is that there are unlikely to be any changes in the basic *structure* of the FHA program before 1996. In other words, the deal you can get now is probably very close to the one you could get anytime before 1996.

The major breakthroughs in this program have just occurred. There aren't likely to be any new ones for a while. If you wait, the only program improvement you are likely to see is the introduction of an equity preservation feature.

Waiting could mean greater loan advances in the future, however, as you become older and if your home's value increases. But a sharp increase in loan costs could reduce or erase that advantage.

Coming Breakthroughs

The next breakthroughs are most likely to occur in the structure and design of lender-insured mortgages.

Two new companies are developing products that are expected to differ from previous ones in up to three ways:

- ◆ you receive monthly advances for as long as you live, *wherever* you live;

- ◆ you *always* have some equity left at the end of the loan; and

- ◆ the loan is structured to be an attractive investment for large institutional investors such as pension funds and insurance companies.

The basic idea is to create a more conservative product for both the borrower and the institutional investor. Greater certainty and less speculation are the goals of these product development efforts.

Whether or not all of these loan features and objectives can be successfully combined remains to be seen. But even at this point, some comments are in order.

Breaking Through What?

If monthly advances continue for life, you may or may not have greater financial security. Much will depend on the *amount* of the advances. And of course you should not forget to figure out the *cost* of the advances, including the amount of leftover equity.

You would expect lifetime advances to be less than tenure advances. If they are, the issue is "how *much* less?". If they aren't, the question is "why not?".

The reason you would expect the monthly advances to be less is that they are guaranteed for a longer period of time. Moreover, if the provider of these mortgage funds is a more conservative investor, this could lower the advances as well.

Apples to Apples

If the lifetime reverse mortgage provides a lower monthly advance, you can compare it to the tenure reverse mortgage in this way:

☐ reduce the amount of the tenure advance down to the level of the lifetime advance, and use the reduction to create an equity reserve, credit-line, or initial lump sum, whichever provides the greatest long-term benefit;

☐ making various assumptions about the term of the loan and the appreciation rate, figure out how much equity you would have left under each plan; and

☐ compare your leftover equity, and estimate how much income it could earn for you.

You might find out, for example, that the lifetime plan could leave you with a net monthly annuity income that is far less than what you could generate with the equity leftover from a tenure plan. If the lifetime plan provides a *much lower* monthly advance, that could well be the case.

Net Advances

Because lifetime plans include an annuity (see next page), you also have to take into account the taxability of annuity payments. It's the after-tax amount you should be comparing to non-taxable loan advances.

Moreover, if you receive SSI, medicaid, or other public benefits, you must consider that annuity payments usually *are* counted as income. They can reduce your cash benefits dollar-for-dollar, or make you ineligible altogether. Again, it's the net amount that counts.

Higher Advances?

But what if the lifetime advances are greater than the tenure advances - even after taxes and benefit reductions? Wouldn't that make it a better deal?

Not necessarily. It might mean much greater costs for some borrowers. For example, the higher advances could be paid for by charging short-lived borrowers more than they would pay in a tenure plan.

That may be just fine with you. It may be exactly the type of deal you want. But you would surely want to know that the loan you select is the one you want.

Figuring out the pattern of TLC rates and leftover equity is the best way of seeing just what you are buying - and at what potential costs. Setting the advances on two different loans at the same level is a good way of comparing apples to apples.

A Reverse *Annuity* Mortgage

Both of the lifetime plans currently being developed involve an annuity.

An annuity is a contract to send you a fixed amount of money every month for the rest of your life. It is a financial product sold by an insurance company.

In a lifetime reverse mortgage, a lump sum advance at closing is used to buy a "deferred" annuity in your name. "Deferred" means that the monthly annuity payments to you do not begin until some specific time in the future.

Up until that time, the lender sends you a loan advance every month. In the month after you receive your last loan advance, your annuity begins, and continues for the rest of your life.

The amount of the monthly loan advance and the amount of the monthly annuity payment are the same. In this way, you get a fixed amount of cash every month from closing until you die - no matter where you live.

Annuities Aren't Loans

When you switch from loan advances to annuity payments, your money starts coming from a different source. Instead of getting cash from a lender, you start getting it from an insurance company.

The lender will be repaid in the future from the equity in your home. But the insurance company has already been paid with a loan advance from your reverse mortgage.

If a lender stops making loan advances, the lender may not get fully repaid. And you still own the home from which repayment must come. If it's an FHA loan, the federal government will continue your loan advances, and deal with the lender.

But what happens if the insurance company providing your annuity fails to perform?

Being Sure of the Insurer

The main question most people have about annuities is safety. How sure can you be that you will get your money?

This is not an idle concern.

Many people remember the failure of Baldwin United in 1983, then one of the largest writers of deferred annuities in America. More recently, pensioners have been shocked by the massive collapse of Executive Life, which sells annuities to pension funds.

You can assess the financial strength of an insurance company by checking its ratings. Go to a library and ask for the rating guides published by A.M. Best, Moody's, Standard and Poor's, and Duff & Phelps.

Or call Standard & Poor's rating desk at 212-208-1527 for free ratings on up to three companies. Moody's rating desk can be reached at 212-553-1653. The A. M. Best rating desk (900-420-0400) charges $2.50 per minute.

You also might ask the insurance company selling the annuity if it is licensed to do business in the state of New York. Many companies are not. Think it has anything to do with New York's reputation for tough regulation of insurance companies?

"State" Guaranty "Funds"

Check to see if your state has a guaranty fund that would protect the specific type of annuity you are being offered.

If it does, ask some questions. Are there dollar limits on the coverage for consumers? Are there percentage limits on the amounts the fund can generate from insurance companies?

These "state funds" are not run by state governments, and they do not have any. Funds, that is. They are run by the insurance industry, and they are empty - *without* funds - until some insurer goes belly up. Then they pass the hat.

The company offering you an annuity and your state legislative representatives should be able to help you get the information you need. But don't stop there. Ask questions. Get the answers in writing.

Annuity Acuity

Financial stability isn't the only issue with annuities. There are also important legal concerns.

You need to make sure that the company selling you an annuity doesn't turn around and sell your account to a less viable company. The best way to do that is to insist that a right to refuse a new carrier be written into your annuity contract.

Another issue is the payment amount. Is it truly guaranteed for as long as you live? Or is the guarantee only good for a few years, after which the insurance company may change the payment amount? Be certain the contract requires the dollar amount to remain the same every month with no exceptions - especially ones that are "never used."

Comparing Future Loan Plans

The best method for analyzing any new plan that appears in the future is to

✓ ask the "three little questions" discussed in Chapters 11 through 16;

✓ explore the issues raised in Chapter 17; and

✓ compare your findings about the new plan with the information on the currently available plans examined in Chapters 18 through 24.

Chapter 30

Sketches of Shoppers

Practice may not make perfect, but it does make better. So before going shopping on your own, you might want to tag along with some people considering reverse mortgages in this chapter. Each short sketch is followed by a brief discussion of the issues it raises.

There are no "correct" answers for these situations. Every real-life story is unique and more complicated than these vignettes can describe. But give it a try. How do your general reactions compare with the comments and questions in the discussion sections? Do you see yourself or anyone else in these stories?

Newly Retired

Mary and John Green have just retired at ages 63 and 66, respectively.

Their joint income is enough to meet their regular monthly needs, and their savings are enough to cover most other expenses that come along. A big part of that income, however, is a pension that will stop when John dies. They own their home free and clear of debt, and expect it would sell for about $80,000.

The Greens have heard about reverse mortgages, and they are very interested. They are thinking about

☐ boosting their monthly income so they can afford more "extras"; or maybe even

☐ getting $20,000 to buy the sporty car Mr. Green has always wanted.

Discussion

By how much will Mary's income drop if John dies before she does? Will her income and savings be enough if he dies five years from now? Ten years from now? Fifteen years?

How much could the Greens actually get from a reverse mortgage? At 10% interest and 4% closing costs, they could get about $150 per month on a tenure basis *OR* about $17,500 in a one-time lump sum from the FHA program.

(Because they are not both at least 65 years old, they do not presently qualify for the Capital Holding plan.)

The basic choice appears to be between

◆ living *somewhat* more comfortably now on an extra $150 per month;

◆ buying a *somewhat* less sporty car than John had wanted; or

◆ forgetting about a reverse mortgage for now, and keeping the home free of debt until a more serious need arises, such as Mary's income if John predeceases her, or any unanticipated major expense or financial emergency.

In short, the Greens probably will decide they are too young for a reverse mortgage at this time. If they use up all their equity now, they won't have it when their need for it is likely to be greater.

Recently Widowed

When Emma Black's husband died three years ago, she wasn't sure what to do.

Her sister wanted Emma to move to her retirement community in another state. Her former neighbor wanted Emma to move into her apartment building. But Emma took her time and put off any decisions.

Turned out to be a smart idea. The more she thought about it, and the more she looked into other possibilities, the more she wanted just to stay put.

Her health was good. She enjoyed her home, her garden, and her neighborhood. She really liked being a homeowner, and taking care of her house.

The only problem was the cost of it all. She was still learning to cope with the loss of her husband's pension. Emma had checked into some government programs, but found that her income - about $11,000 - was too high for her to qualify.

She had heard about reverse mortgages, but didn't think much about them until two things happened:

✓ she read about a new federal insurance program that guarantees reverse mortgages; and

✓ a home like hers just a few blocks away sold for $100,000.

At age 75, Emma had no one who needed to inherit her home. But she was very cautious about financial matters. Her husband had always handled their affairs, and now she couldn't afford to make any mistakes.

Yes, it would be nice to get some money out of her home *and* live in it. But she had never expected to be taking out a new type of mortgage in her mid-70s.

What Emma Black liked very much, therefore, was the idea of a program guaranteed by the federal government.

Discussion

Has Emma Black investigated *all* the government programs for which she may be eligible? Has she considered the other options in Chapter 26?

What are Emma's specific needs? What types of loan advances would best fit her situation?

How much could she get from the FHA program? Is the Capital Holding plan available in her area? Her age and home value are the same as the examples presented in Chapters 21, 24, and 27.

Just how much is the federal guarantee worth to Emma Black? Would she rather have the flexibility and government guarantee of the FHA program even if it provides less cash? How much less?

Fixing to Fix

Ethel White has been fixing to fix her roof and front porch for almost a year. She's 81, so she's seen a few of each come and go.

Trouble is, she can't ever seem to save enough. And her income is too low to qualify for one of those "home equity" loans.

Ethel expects the repairs will cost about $3,500. And that's more than half her annual income. She has managed to save nearly $2,000. But the property taxes on her $75,000 debt-free home will soon be due, and that will use up about half her savings.

317

Discussion

With an annual income under $7,000, Ethel White could be eligible for some of the income programs discussed in Chapter 26.

She is probably also eligible for a home repair grant, deferred payment loan, or property tax deferral. If they are offered in her area, these programs may be all she would choose to do at this time.

Or, she could consider also taking a private reverse mortgage to supplement her monthly income. If she does, she should check to see if the public loan programs would agree to take second position behind the private loan.

If there are no public programs, she could consider a private loan with a monthly income plan and a lump sum at closing to cover her repair costs.

Looking for Credit

Income is not Peter Gray's problem.

He isn't wealthy. But then he has no trouble making ends meet each month either. His regular income allows him to live comfortably at age 72.

The problem is this home equity loan he's been carrying for years. It's got a high interest rate, and he'd like to be out from under it once and for all. The thought of "no more payments" is very attractive.

There's also this home improvement he's been thinking about for a long time. Sure would make life more comfortable and enjoyable.

And then there's his worries. Calls them his "what if's." As in "what if the furnace gives out" or "what if I need some in-home help."

And finally, there's his dreams: a first-class trip to the old country, a complete new computer system.

What's been fueling all these thoughts has been the rise in Peter Gray's home equity. It's slowed down some recently. But the run-up was so strong for so long that even a fallback would leave him far ahead.

And yet he can't imagine selling and moving. He'd gladly give up all the items on his list if that were the only way he could remain in his home.

Discussion

Does Peter Gray sound like a candidate for a creditline reverse mortgage? Too bad if he does.

Only the FHA offers a standalone line-of-credit. And Peter's home is worth much more than the FHA's 203-b-2 limit in his area. He's still eligible for the FHA plan. But the amount he can get from it is very limited relative to the equity he holds.

Peter can's see encumbering all or most of his equity in order to get at a minor part of it. So he decides to wait until America's financial services industry figures out how to meet his needs. Stay tuned.

Needing Some Help

Because she'd always been so independent and energetic, it was hard for Betty Brown to deal with the effects of her recently-diagnosed chronic illness.

The hardest part was needing the help of others to do the things she'd always done for herself. She was still living in her own home, but she could no longer handle everything all by herself.

Betty was also having trouble figuring out all the ins and outs of arranging for the services she needed - and paying for them. She'd been responsible for some intricate budgets in her time, but none of it could hold a candle to the complexities she now faced.

When she found an experienced case manager, things improved quickly. As some order was imposed on her new world chaos, Betty started to feel much better.

It was then that she began to focus on the financial aspects of her situation. She would need more money. And the amount needed would vary from time to time.

The case manager had done a good job of maximizing all the other available resources. Now Betty would have to generate some funds.

The fact that she owned a home free of debt gave her some extra room to maneuver. Her first thought was a home equity loan. Her case manager suggested they also look into reverse mortgages.

Discussion

The first thing Betty Brown found was that her new financial situation made her a poor candidate for a home equity loan. Simply put, she could no longer qualify for one.

The second thing she found was that only the FHA reverse mortgage was available in her area. But it was so flexible and adaptable that it fit her situation very well.

Paying for in-home and community services is a common use of reverse mortgages. Like others before her, Betty Brown discovered that you can use your home equity to help you stay in your home.

Avoiding Eviction

William Ivory was in bad shape.

Soon after his wife died, his health deteriorated rapidly. Worse, he started losing contact with the few people he knew. In time, he began neglecting his own health and nutritional needs.

So William was in no condition to deal with the serious furnace and plumbing problems that erupted in the same cold January week.

And he hadn't even been opening the legal notices he had been receiving about his failure to pay property taxes, and repay a home equity loan.

By the time a local social services agency became involved, William was delusional, malnourished, and on the verge of eviction from his home.

Discussion

None of it was easy.

But for a while the hardest part appeared to be holding on to the home.

The furnace and plumbing problems had become building code violations, and the local deferred payment loan program had run out of funds. William's tax delinquency included a substantial special assessment, and there was no tax deferral program. The home equity loan was well past due, and the lender was foreclosing on it.

All that stood between William and the street was a lump sum of cash to make the repairs, pay off the taxes, and repay the home equity loan.

As it happened, one lender in the large urban area in which William lived had just started making FHA-insured reverse mortgages. That one, forward-looking lender had decided to meet the credit needs of the retired homeowning community.

And one social services agency had decided to learn about reverse mortgages.

Luckily for William Ivory, the connections got made, and he kept his home. It was only one part of his overall needs, but an essential one.

Adding Life to Years?

Nan and Dan Silver feel blessed.

In their early seventies, they are financially comfortable and in great physical shape. They have enough to live on each month, and a substantial nest egg for future contingencies.

They have always been very disciplined when it comes to money. Right now they could be dipping into their savings and investments in order to do more things. But they have always followed a "safety-first" approach, and see no reason to stop.

The Silvers' top financial priority is to keep more than enough funds in reserve to meet future needs. And if that means living more modestly now, then so be it. They would rather die rich than take any chance of running out.

The Neighbors

Their neighbors, George and Martha Gold, could not agree more. In fact, their financial situation is almost exactly the same as the Silvers'. They are in their mid-seventies.

But just last week, George - a retired banker - was reading about these new reverse mortgages. And it got him to thinking.

Without any heirs, he and Martha had no one who would inherit their nest egg or their home. If they took

323

out a reverse mortgages they wouldn't have any trouble figuring out what to do with an extra check in the mail every month.

Meanwhile, they could keep their nest egg safe while living more comfortably and doing more things. Hadn't they earned that much?

The Discussion

Well you should have heard it. When Nan and Dan and George and Martha got together for bridge, it just went on and on.

George introduced the subject while Nan watched Dan's reaction. Dan thought it was a foolish idea. Why go back into debt? Hadn't they all worked hard to pay off their mortgages? Why even think about taking out a new mortgage at their ages?

Different Debt?

George said it was a different kind of debt with a different purpose. There weren't any monthly payments to make, and you could boost your income without touching your savings and investments. Besides, homes aren't going to keep appreciating anywhere near as much as they have been. So why not turn that risk over to someone else?

But Dan just couldn't see it. They hadn't been financially disciplined their whole lives only to go wobbly in their later years. This was no time even to consider putting debt against their homes.

324

George told him he wouldn't think so if he didn't have three kids, eight grandkids, and eleven great grandkids. If you had no heirs like us, said George, you'd be whistling a different tune.

But Dan said that had nothing to do with it. Most of their heirs were in fantastic financial shape. The Silvers weren't keeping all their powder dry primarily for their kids' sake. They were doing it for themselves. It was the prudent thing to do.

That's when it started to get a little more lively.

"Does prudence *ever* become hoarding?" George asked. "Is *no* amount of savings 'enough'? Isn't your home now worth ten times what you paid for it? Can't you think of *anything* you could do with that windfall equity? Besides sit on it and count it, that is?"

But before Dan could answer, Nan went back to the issue of heirs.

Guests and Bequests

"You know," she said, "Not all of our kids are in great financial shape all the time. Now and then it would be nice to be able to help them out more. And I sure would like to visit our grandkids more often. It would be easier to have them visit us if we put on that addition we've talked about."

Then she added, "Sometimes I think about what they will inherit, and I'd sure rather be around when they get some of it so we can enjoy it with them."

That quieted things down for a bit.

When Martha broke the silence, it was to ask George just what he thought they would spend the extra money from a reverse mortgage on. (Not that she didn't have a few ideas herself.)

Martha had been a little surprised by George's interest in reverse mortgages. He had always been very conservative in their financial dealings. But he was also always on the lookout for better ways of doing things. Martha was just curious about his plans for the cash. So were the Silvers.

How About You?

Congratulations! You've done it. You've made it all the way through to the last drop. You are now one of the few people in America who knows something about reverse mortgages.

As an informed consumer, you are the essential ingredient in the development of this market. Only you can decide if any of these loans make sense for you - now, or in the future. Only you can judge which plan does the best job of meeting your unique needs. Only you can effectively demand these programs from the lending community.

So do me a favor. Keep in touch. Let me know what you see and learn. Tell me what's happening or not happening in your area. And, in particular, let me know if you hear about a reverse mortgage borrower with more than 87 rosebushes.

326

Appendixes

Appendix A: Calculating Total Loan Cost Rates

Example (FHA loan):
- ☐ Duration of loan = 12 years
- ☐ Advances = $351.93 per month
- ☐ Amount owed after 12 years = $115,706

Keystrokes (Hewlett-Packard 12C):
- ☐ f CLEAR FIN 12 g 12X (144)
- ☐ 351.93 CHS PMT (-351.93)
- ☐ 115,706 FV (115,706)
- ☐ g BEG i (1.02266747)
- ☐ g 12X = 12.27200963

Appendix B: FHA Principal Limit Factors

Age	8%	9%	10%	11%	12%	13%	14%
62	0.371	0.302	0.247	0.204	0.17	0.143	0.122
63	0.381	0.313	0.258	0.214	0.179	0.151	0.129
64	0.393	0.324	0.268	0.224	0.188	0.159	0.136
65	0.405	0.336	0.28	0.234	0.197	0.168	0.144
66	0.417	0.348	0.291	0.245	0.208	0.177	0.153
67	0.429	0.36	0.303	0.257	0.218	0.187	0.162
68	0.442	0.373	0.316	0.268	0.23	0.198	0.171
69	0.454	0.386	0.329	0.281	0.241	0.208	0.181

Age	8%	9%	10%	11%	12%	13%	14%
70	0.467	0.4	0.342	0.294	0.254	0.22	0.192
71	0.481	0.413	0.356	0.307	0.267	0.232	0.203
72	0.494	0.428	0.37	0.321	0.28	0.245	0.215
73	0.508	0.442	0.385	0.336	0.294	0.258	0.228
74	0.522	0.457	0.4	0.351	0.309	0.273	0.241
75	0.537	0.472	0.416	0.367	0.324	0.287	0.256
76	0.551	0.488	0.432	0.383	0.34	0.303	0.27
77	0.566	0.504	0.448	0.399	0.356	0.319	0.286
78	0.581	0.52	0.465	0.417	0.373	0.335	0.302
79	0.596	0.536	0.482	0.434	0.391	0.353	0.319
80	0.611	0.553	0.5	0.452	0.409	0.371	0.336
81	0.626	0.569	0.517	0.47	0.427	0.389	0.354
82	0.641	0.586	0.535	0.488	0.446	0.408	0.373
83	0.656	0.603	0.553	0.507	0.465	0.427	0.392
84	0.671	0.619	0.571	0.526	0.484	0.446	0.412
85	0.686	0.636	0.589	0.545	0.504	0.466	0.432
86	0.7	0.652	0.607	0.564	0.524	0.486	0.452
87	0.715	0.668	0.624	0.583	0.543	0.507	0.473
88	0.729	0.685	0.642	0.602	0.564	0.528	0.494
89	0.743	0.701	0.66	0.621	0.584	0.549	0.516
90	0.757	0.717	0.678	0.641	0.605	0.571	0.539
95	0.832	0.805	0.778	0.751	0.725	0.7	0.675

Glossary

annuity - a monthly payment for life

appreciation - an increase in the value of a home

appraisal - an estimate of a home's market value

closing - a meeting at which legal documents are signed to "close the deal" on a mortgage; the time at which a mortgage begins

creditline - see *line-of-credit*

default - the failure of a borrower or lender to fulfill agreed-upon mortgage terms

deferred payment loans - reverse mortgages providing lump sums of cash for repairing or improving homes

depreciation - a decrease in the value of a home

expected interest rate - in the FHA program, a constant interest rate used to calculate loan advances

FHA - the Federal Housing Administration, which is part of the U.S. Department of Housing and Urban Development (HUD)

FHA reverse mortgage insurance - a reverse mortgage insurance program authorized by Congress and administered by the FHA

FHA-insured reverse mortgages - insured reverse mortgages in which the FHA prescribes the advances and retains most or all of the insurance premiums

home equity - the value of a home minus any debt against it

home equity conversion - turning home equity into cash without having to leave your home or make regular loan repayments

home equity conversion mortgage - a reverse mortgage loan

Home Equity Conversion Mortgage (HECM) Insurance Demonstration Program - the FHA reverse mortgage insurance program

insured reverse mortgages - reverse mortgages in which insurance premiums are charged to cover the risk of loan losses

joint tenancy - equal ownership rights held by two or more persons that survive the death of any owner

lender-insured reverse mortgages - insured reverse mortgages in which lenders prescribe the advances and retain the insurance premiums

lump sum - a single loan advance of a substantial amount

line-of-credit - a credit account that permits a borrower to control the timing and amount of the loan advances

loan advances - payments made by a lender to a borrower, or to another party on behalf of a borrower

loan balance - the amount owed, including principal and interest; limited in a reverse mortgage by a non-recourse feature

loan term - the period of time from closing until the loan is due and payable

maximum claim amount - in the FHA program, the appraised value of the home OR the 203-b-2 limit, whichever is less

mortgage - a legal document making a home available to a lender to satisfy a debt

non-recourse mortgage - a loan in which a lender may only look to the value of the home for repayment

origination - the administrative process of setting up a mortgage, including the preparation of documents

principal - see *loan advances*

principal limit - in the FHA program, the largest amount of cash a borrower could receive at closing; used to calculate other loan advance amounts

property tax deferrals - reverse mortgages providing annual loan advances for paying property taxes

reverse annuity mortgage - a reverse mortgage in which a lump sum at closing is used to purchase an annuity

reverse mortgage - a loan against home equity providing loan advances to a borrower and requiring no repayment until a future time

sale leaseback - the sale of a home to a buyer who immediately rents it back to the seller on a long-term lease

servicing - performing administrative functions on a loan after closing

tenure advances - fixed monthly advances for as long as a borrower lives in a home

term advances - fixed monthly advances for a specific period of time

Total Loan Cost (TLC) - the projected annual average cost of a reverse mortgage including all loan costs as limited by the non-recourse feature

Truth-in-Lending - the federal law that requires full disclosure of charges and terms prior to closing, and provides a 3-day right of written cancellation after closing

uninsured reverse mortgages - reverse mortgages in which no insurance premium is charged to cover the risk of loan losses

Resources

Chapter 2 - Beginnings

Scholen, Ken. **Reverse Mortgage Sourcebook,** National Center for Home Equity Conversion (NCHEC), Marshall MN, 1991

Scholen, Ken and Yung-Ping Chen (eds.). **Unlocking Home Equity for the Elderly,** Ballinger Publishing, Cambridge MA, 1981

Chapter 17 - On the Lookout

American Association of Retired Persons (AARP). **Model State Law on Reverse Mortgages,** Washington DC, 1990

Chapter 18 - Deferred Payment Loans

Perkins, William C. **DPL Program Development Handbook,** NCHEC, Marshall MN, 1984

Chapter 21 - FHA Program: Benefits

U.S. Department of Housing and Urban Development, **Home Equity Conversion Mortgages; Handbook 4235.1,** Washington DC, 1989

Chapter 25 - To Thine Own Self

Weaver, Peter and Annette Buchanon. **What To Do With What You've Got: The Practical Guide to Money Management in Retirement,** AARP, Washington DC, 1989

Chapter 26 - Other Options

AARP. **Thrive and Survive: AARP's Guide to Financial Resource Publications** (D13073), Washington DC

Ernst, Trudy and Maurice Weinrobe. **Sale Lease-back Guide and Model Documents**, NCHEC, Marshall MN 1983

Fullner, Wanda. **Women: Take Charge of Your Money** (D13183), AARP, Washington DC, 1988

Hobbs, Robert J. **Borrowing Against Your Home: The Risks, Pitfalls, and Advantages of Home Equity Loans** (D12987), AARP, Washington DC, 1988,

Salmen, John. **The Do-Able Renewable Home** (D12470), AARP, Washington DC, 1988

United Seniors Health Cooperative. **Long-Term Care: A Dollar and Sense Guide**, Washington DC, 1991

Chapter 28 - Other Financial Effects

American Bar Association. **Attorney's Guide to Home Equity Conversion**, Commission on Legal Problems of the Elderly, Washington DC, 1991

Chapter 29 - Looking Ahead

NCHEC. **Designing Reverse Mortgages: Technical Papers,** Marshall MN, 1991

Index

About the Author

Ken Scholen founded and directs the National Center for Home Equity Conversion. Since 1978, he has promoted the development of reverse mortgages on a fulltime basis through research, training, consulting, publishing, public relations, and public policy analysis and advocacy. He edited the first book (1981), organized the first national conferences (1979, 1983), and conducted the first public research projects (1978-84) in the field.

Scholen has presented testimony to four committees of Congress, and has keynoted conferences and led training sessions in 35 states. He has consulted with most of the reverse mortgage development efforts in the United States, and some in England, Canada, Spain, Australia, and Japan. He has also been a consultant to the U. S. Senate Special Committee on Aging, the U. S. Administration on Aging, American Bar Association, National Council of State Housing Agencies, National Association of State Units on Aging, and the Canadien Association on Gerontology.

He helped establish - and since 1985 has served as a consultant to - AARP's Home Equity Information Center. He has authored consumer guides for AARP, HUD, and NCHEC. More than 250,000 copies of his publications are currently in print.

Scholen originated the FHA reverse mortgage insurance proposal (1981), assisted in drafting the initial legislation (1983), authored key technical amendments (1985-87), led the effort to gain Congressional approval (1983-87), consulted with HUD in designing the program (1988), and trained 1,500 FHA consumer counselors, private lenders, and HUD staff members (1989-91).

In other areas, Scholen has directed a state board on aging, co-founded a statewide senior advocacy coalition, developed an innovative senior housing facility, directed a comprehensive senior services organization, conducted research in city government, and lobbied for six years on child welfare issues. He was a founding board member of United Seniors Health Cooperative (DC) and the Wisconsin Partnership for Housing Development.

About NCHEC

The National Center for Home Equity Conversion is an independent, not-for-profit organization devoted to the development of sound home equity conversion opportunities for homeowners.

NCHEC conducts educational seminars for consumers, counselors, and consumer organizations. It provides research and consultation services for product and program developers, public policymakers, and the media. The Center collects and publishes a variety of materials, serving as a national clearinghouse on reverse mortgages and other home equity conversion plans.

NCHEC received start-up funding from the Florence V. Burden Foundation (NY), the Retirement Research Foundation (IL), the Levi Strauss Foundation (CA), and the Kimberly Clark Foundation (WI). Its ongoing support has come primarily from federal and state government research and training grants, consulting work with consumer organizations, and sales of publications. Established in 1981 in Madison, Wisconsin, the Center grew out of state and federal research projects on home equity conversion. NCHEC moved to Minnesota (1210 East College - Suite 300, Marshall MN 56258; 507-532-3230) in 1989.

Other NCHEC Publications

Reverse Mortgage Sourcebook - itemized history of reverse mortgage development; current market statistics; federal laws and regulations; bibliography of published and unpublished papers, articles, and other materials; directory of current programs

Sale Leaseback Guide and Model Documents - a legal and financial guide to structuring sale leaseback transactions; includes sample legal documents with section-by-section narrative

Designing Reverse Mortgages: Technical Papers - seminal research reports that led to key breakthroughs in the development of risk-sharing reverse mortgage instruments